High Notes and Low

High Notes and Low

✦

Recollections of a Musical Career
(with Strings attached)

Esther Schure Gilbert

iUniverse, Inc.
New York Lincoln Shanghai

High Notes and Low
Recollections of a Musical Career (with Strings attached)

iUniverse books may be ordered through booksellers or by contacting:

iUniverse
2021 Pine Lake Road, Suite 100
Lincoln, NE 68512
www.iuniverse.com
1-800-Authors (1-800-288-4677)

ISBN-13: 978-0-595-41875-6 (pbk)
ISBN-13: 978-0-595-67948-5 (cloth)
ISBN-13: 978-0-595-86222-1 (ebk)
ISBN-10: 0-595-41875-9 (pbk)
ISBN-10: 0-595-67948-X (cloth)
ISBN-10: 0-595-86222-5 (ebk)

Contents

Acknowledgements

I have been fortunate in my friendships over the years. I especially want to recognize Hazel Stern, Rochester, New York. She was my patroness and underwrote the cost of my first fine violin. She worked tirelessly to promote my career.

In Huntsville, Alabama, since my retirement I have been encouraged by Dr. Reese Kilgo, Barbara Lapidus (a very special and dedicated friend), and Bill Snoddy—tops among many. When my "memoirs" get into print it will be through their interest and effort. There are no words that can adequately express my appreciation for all they have done and continue to do.

I should say a gigantic, loving "thank you" to my family. Their ongoing support for anything I choose to do is a comfort and an inspiration. Thank you, dear Michael, Dr. Stephen, Dr. Richard and their families, and my brother, Dr. Alexander Schure (my number one fan since day one.) Also, kudos to my nephew, Louis Schure, for saving these treasured photos and making them available to the publisher.

Mother

First Lessons

From my earliest recollections I hear my mother's voice. She is singing to me. The words, in Yiddish, are about a little violin—what sweet music it can make—and urge me to ask my father to buy the little violin for me. Often, involved in some activity, I would say, "Mama, don't sing." But she persisted and, eventually, found a tiny violin for me.

Small as the violin was, it was too big for me. My Uncle Dave, the Russian-trained musician, decided it would be wise to wait until I was at least four years old before starting lessons.

The important birthday arrived at last. I had grown sufficiently so that I could handle the violin. Very soon after that my mother took me, along with the violin, bow, and case, to my uncle for my first lesson. He taught me how to hold the violin and the bow, told me the names of the four strings and, finally, let me draw the bow across the strings. After a few minutes, he sat down at the piano and began to play wonderful, shifting chords under each open string. I felt as though I were in the midst of a color explosion. From that moment, I knew I had to learn to play.

My uncle gave me a lecture on the importance of practicing, of listening, and of aiming for high standards. I could hardly wait to begin.

Subsequent lessons went well. I was making good progress. One day we arrived at his house to find him in an angry mood. He was, as I recall, a vain and selfish man. Evidently, he had had another of the many arguments between him and my Aunt Sophie. As a result he was very impatient with me, scolded, raised his voice and, in general, discouraged me. As we left his house I turned to my mother and said, "If you want me to play the violin *you* have to find me a nice lady teacher who doesn't holler."

Thus it was that I began lessons at the Hamilton Conservatory with Miss Martha Slater, a very nice lady who didn't holler.

Recollections of My Father

When I was three my father began teaching me the alphabet. It started as a whim of his but soon became a nightly, after supper routine. Our only prop was a huge bag of wooden clothespins. My father would draw an A, then I would make another A with the clothes pins. I can still recall the frustration of trying to make a C or Q or S with the non-bendable clothespins. I tried to explain the problem to my father but he dismissed my desire, even then, for accuracy and perfection. "Use your imagination," he would say. "Don't be a stick-in-the-mud."

My father came to Canada as a young Jewish immigrant. He had fled czarist Russia to avoid being conscripted into the army, and to see for himself what opportunities were to be found in the New World. For years he told stories of strange and terrible things that happened in the army—particularly to young Jewish boys. He was one of the few from his "gibernee-eh" (a district or large area) who was permitted to attend school. I can recall his reading the Hamilton (Ontario) *The Spectator* newspaper every day from first page to last—discussing the various articles in detail. Many were the times I went to school and shared some of these discussions with my teacher and fellow students.

Inasmuch as my Father's English was largely self-taught, there were many words whose pronunciations were strictly his own. The example that comes to mind most clearly was his comment, after a lengthy discourse, that there was "a crizziss in Yahpohne-eh". I recall clearly the mystified look on the teacher's face. Then she said, "Oh, you mean a crisis in Japan?" I replied that my pronunciation was exactly as my father's had been. "I'm sure your father is a very nice man," she said, "but the correct pronunciation is "a crisis in Japan." I never told my father about the incident.

He was always reminding us of the value of good manners, of respectful behavior, of speaking clearly, without verbal mannerisms. Most of all, he urged us to avoid "vuglarity." (sic)

Our family observed the Jewish Sabbath which begins Friday evenings. For as long as she was able, my mother always set the Sabbath table with a freshly laundered white cloth and gleaming, silver candlesticks. My father read the Bible explaining the laws and philosophies of the service. After dinner he would read to us again, often stories by Sholom Aleichem. He added comments that enhanced the reading, helping us understand the times and the hardships of the characters.

The flaw in my father's character was his temper. I suppose if psychology were as much a part of one's knowledge as it is today, he might have been able to control it better. I can understand, too, the frustration for a man of his intelligence to have to settle for a job he disliked, provide for a growing family, and abandon his youthful dreams. One never knew when or what would disturb or offend or displease him. The results were always the same—high decibel shouting, pounding on the table or desk, occasional threats of physical harm. The resulting stress did little for my nervous system or my desperate longing for serenity. Much later, when my sister and brother married, their homes were models of cheerful surroundings and havens of peace.

I owe my dislike of waste—in any form—to my father's examples. Since times were very hard there were rarely any opportunities to spend money freely. We were taught that obligations—bills, rent, dues, taxes—were the first priority. Much later in his life, when he managed to accumulate property amd money, he became generous; to charities, to his temple, and to many other causes he felt deserved assistance. He learned to enjoy his grandchildren. He made trips to Florida for occasional vacations. He even traveled to Israel. The card he sent us read, "This place is a miracle."

When he emigrated from Russia, he landed in Halifax, Nova Scotia. Once past the immigration hurdles he proceeded to London, Ontario. He had the address of some distant relatives—later my maternal grandparents. They welcomed him with controlled enthusiasm and found out all they needed to know about his education, his hopes and plans. He told them he hoped to go to college and learn some worthy skills such as teaching or writing. These ambitions were promptly dismissed—he had to find a job, they told him, get married, and learn to enjoy practical things. He met their daughter, Bess, and it was taken for granted they would soon be married.

Meanwhile, he was told, there was a great opportunity for him to learn how to be a good cigar maker. Thus began many years of frustration for my father. He hated being a cigar maker—although he became a skilled maker of the most expensive cigars—Panatellas, Coronas, and other fancy shapes. He never smoked. Occasionally he had to light a cigar and take a few puffs to make sure the cigar would "draw." It was always a trying experience to witness these "tests"—the shouting, the language, the spitting, and, occasionally, the curses—(very impressive in Russian).

My family joined the conservative Temple. Very soon after that my father became a member of the men's club and attended the Sunday morning meetings with much more enthusiasm than he showed at the regular services. I learned my first *big* word that first Sunday when he came home from the meeting and announced that the name of the men's club was, officially, "The Hebrew Benevolent Society." Their purpose was to raise funds to help local widows and orphans, and perhaps other worthy causes. I asked him about the meaning of "benevolent." After his explanation, the word promptly became part of my vocabulary.

He was not given to expressions of endearment or to lavish praise. A promise was a commitment. He made his displeasure clear when promises were not kept, or taken lightly. He urged us to enjoy the outdoors, to be aware of the endless variety in nature—of shapes and colors, of insects, birds, and animals.

His ultimate advice was that education was the key to a worthy life. "You want to be somebody?" he would ask. "Study! Learn to do something better than anybody else."

Hamilton, Ontario

Grandma Bahsheh

Until I was ten years old my home was in Hamilton, Canada. My first address was 102 Napier Street, a modest house next to a large steelwire factory. The neighborhood was part Italian and part Jewish. My school, Hess Street School, was a few blocks from our house.

My father's parents lived at 14 Crooks Street, which afforded a glimpse of Lake Ontario a couple of blocks away. My mother's parents lived in London, Ontario, at least fifty miles away. As a result we saw much more of my father's family in my early years. Several of my uncles lived at home—all busy trying to find work, learn the English language and the English ways. There were seven boys and one girl—all émigrés from Russia. How my parents managed to bring them to Canada was a saga in itself ... filial responsibility, self-deprivation, except for the most basic necessities, endless hours of work, and saving every possible penny.

It must have been a difficult adjustment for all of them, especially the older people. Yet I never heard any one of them say he missed the old country nor considered going back. My grandmother was cheerful, hard-working and non-complaining despite burdens that would have brought a lesser spirit to despair.

Her only daughter, my Aunt Helen, had always been a tomboy. Once, climbing a tree or a fence she fell and injured herself so severely that she was never able to walk again. My grandmother took her to every doctor, every hospital, to faith healers and hypnotists. She grasped at straws. Nothing was too difficult if it offered the hope of Helen's walking again. It was not to be. Helen died when she was eighteen.

My grandmother turned her energies into experimenting with juices, fruits and vegetables in a desire to make cosmetics. Every inch of shelf space, window-sills, table tops, etc., were covered with bottles, jars, saucers, bowls—all filled with mixtures of lemon, yogurt, spices, and herbs. I don't know whether she ever sold anything. I do know that her skin looked remarkably clear and fresh, well into her old age. It has always been my feeling she was a potential Helena Rubenstein, but born at the wrong time.

She loved hats, the bigger the better—decorated with feathers or flowers. She also loved earrings—long and dangling, bejeweled with colorful stones like chandeliers. She wore them with an aristocratic bearing that lent hats and earrings dignity and elegance.

When I won the All-City medal in a competition, (I was seven or eight, small for my age) she was in the audience. As my name was announced she leaped from her seat in mid-auditorium and made her way onto the stage. She enveloped me in embraces and kisses, then opened the enormous handbag she carried, fished around for a few seconds, and handed me a silver quarter along with additional hugs and kisses. I was very embarrassed by all this display, although the audience loved every moment of it. As soon as we were off the stage I explained to my grandmother that onstage behavior should be quiet and dignified. She paid no attention to me, exuberantly shook hands with everyone backstage, and enjoyed the exciting moments to the full.

Looking back, after more than seventy years, I am truly happy my grandmother was there and able to share the honor and excitement of the occasion.

The Burlesque Show

My Uncle Harry was the fifth of my grandparents' seven boys. He dressed well, was good-looking and popular with the girls. Evenings, and some afternoons, he had a job at the Hamilton Grand Opera House where the fare rarely lived up to the grandeur of the name. Road shows, plays, and an occasional concert were the usual offerings. Most often, and most popular, were the burlesque shows.

My uncle usually had a few house tickets to give to favored friends. If he felt the show was in reasonably good taste he would offer the tickets to his girl friends. My grandmother, taken in by the Grand Opera House title, was eager to attend and often asked my uncle for tickets. He always had good excuses to turn her down.

One day he offered her three tickets for a show called "Bringing Up Father." My grandmother immediately invited my sister, Alice, and me, age five and six and one-half, to attend. She evidently thought the show was based on the comic strip of the same name and that it would be fun for children.

The day of the performance arrived. My sister and I, dressed in our party clothes, the little silk blouses, the pongee jumpers all hand sewn by our mother and, special of specials, the new patent leather Mary Jane slippers with socks that matched our blouses, accompanied our grandmother to the theater. I didn't see any other children in the audience but I liked the excitement of the crowds, the candy butcher (vendor), and the festive feeling. If Grandma were a more suspicious or sophisticated type she might have noticed that there were mostly men in the audience. She was just as excited as we were—being at a real live show.

Even when the chorus girls trooped onstage in their very skimpy costumes she wasn't suspicious or angry—just upset that the girls might be cold. I watched and listened to everything that went on. Not for nothing was I called "the little pitcher with big ears." Any time there was a strong audience response to an onstage action or remark I promptly memorized it. My sister was more interested in the candy Grandma bought for us.

As soon as we returned home my father wanted to hear all about our afternoon at the theatre. I told him about the crowds and the candy butchers, the music, the dancing, and especially, the comedians. Then I sang him one of the songs accompanied with as much of the dance as I could remember. "Biscuits in the oven, gettin' all brown. Papa's upstairs chasin' Mama all around." My father looked a little startled but before he could say anything I told him a joke I remembered but didn't quite understand. "What? Six men and six women on the Jury? They were locked up all night and they came in with a verdict of "not guilty!"

At that point my father turned livid—ran to the telephone, called my grandmother and yelled, "What are you trying to do to my daughters? Are you daft taking them to see such a bad taste show? Wait till I see that crazy son of yours!"

My sister and I felt sorry to hear our Grandma scolded. We had enjoyed the show, thought it glamorous and grown up. Live and learn.

Toronto

My mother decided, soon after I won the All-Hamilton Medal, that Hamilton's musical opportunities were no longer adequate for my needs. She had heard there was an exceptional teacher in Toronto. His name was Henri Czaplinski. He was on the faculty of the Hamburg Conservatory. She lost no time in making an appointment for me to play for him.

We arrived, via the Toronto-Hamilton-Buffalo railroad, on a Thursday afternoon. I was awed by the old-world glamour of the Hamburg building—huge rooms, very high ceilings, beautiful molding. Most of all, I was impressed with the dozens of autographed pictures of famous artists of the day—Elman, Casals, Caruso, Wall-Curtis, Heifetz, Leopold Auer and Vladimir-de Pachman, among many others.

My first sight of Mr. Czaplinski startled me. He looked like a portrait of Paganini come alive. Very outgoing, he did his best to put me at ease, listened carefully to my playing. Then he came close to me—studied my tiny hands with an expression of disbelief.

"I'll accept her as a student", he said to my mother. "I'll want her at the Conservatory every day. She'll do her practicing here. I'll give her a lesson as often as I can—and check on her practicing several times during the day." I was awarded a scholarship to cover the lesson fee.

My mother arranged for me to stay at my grandparents' home during the week. On weekends I took the train back to Hamilton. Mondays I returned to the Hamburg school for the Monday to Friday routine of practicing and lessons. Usually whenever I had my lesson with Mr. Czaplinski he would have at least half a dozen of his other students come in as auditions. He explained he wanted me to become accustomed to playing before an audience. He asked me to smile more and encouraged me to be more outgoing.

Worried that I was not eating enough, he arranged for milk and crackers to be brought to my practice room at mid-morning. I know he meant well. Unfortunately, I could not digest milk. Today it is an easily recognized condition—lactose intolerance—and easily controlled. Every time I drank the milk I would be ill or in pain. I learned many ways of avoiding this unwanted treat.

All of the train conductors on the Hamilton-Toronto run knew me by sight. (It couldn't have been too difficult. I was seven years old and carried a violin case). Many train passengers brought their lunch and ate it on the train. Once a lady seated next to me, unwrapping a neatly packed lunch, studied me for a moment and then offered me a sandwich. I said "No thank you," but she insisted. "You're much too thin, little girl. You must learn to eat well." I accepted the sandwich. It was very different from any I'd ever seen at home. The bread was evenly and thinly sliced. I knew it was store-bought. At home my mother baked her own braided challah—big and fragrant and always thickly cut.

On the rare occasion when we had store-bought bread at home it came from the one kosher delicatessen in Hamilton, and was either rye or pumpernickel. The sandwich I'd been offered had mayonnaise and thinly sliced pink meat. As soon as I tasted it I knew it was forbidden—non-kosher. I did eat it, but felt guilty for a long time afterward. I really expected to be struck by lightning or some other reminder of disapproval for this infraction. I never told anyone at home about the "trayf" (non-kosher) sandwich I'd eaten.

I stayed at the Hamburg Conservatory for about two years. One day, after a lesson before the usual auditions, I was stopped in the hallway by one of the teachers—an older man with a ruddy complexion. He wanted to ask me something about the concerto I had played that morning. He sat down in a comfortable chair and called me over. I was uneasy in his presence and remained a good distance from him. Suddenly he reached out and pulled me onto his lap. "You're not seven years old" he said. His voice had a strangled sound. His breathing seemed labored. Somehow I got away from him. My heart was pounding—my mouth dry.

I managed to find my coat and left the building without saying anything to anyone. I took the streetcar back to my grandparents' house and did not mention anything to them about the incident.

Nevertheless, next day I could not bring myself to return to my usual routine. I did not go to the Conservatory or call them. It seems strange that my grandparents were unaware of the change in my routine. After several days, my parents called to ask why I was not attending my practicing and my lessons at the school. Apparently the school had contacted them.

"I don't want to go there anymore." "Why not?" "I just don't want to."

My mother wasted no time. Next day she was in Toronto. Before she left to return home she had contacted the officials at the Royal Conservatory and arranged for me to play for Dr. McMillan, president, and Ferdinand Fillion, head of the violin department. I was accepted by Mr. Fillion and began studies with him the next day. Compared to Czaplinski, Fillion was traditional and calm. He was a Belgian trained pedagogue. He gave me two hour-long lessons each week. I took no other classes nor did I play in the Conservatory orchestra. I was awarded a scholarship that took care of the lesson fee.

From my grandparents home on D'Arcy Street I walked the mile or so to the Conservatory. Whatever music I owned was in a large leather bag. I slung the shoulder strap over my left shoulder. My hands were free to take proper care of the violin case. Whenever I was assigned a new work I added it to my backpack collection. It never occurred to me to take a trolley. By the time I reached the Royal College I was probably listing to one side. Winter temperatures being what they are in Toronto, I marvel, in retrospect, that I was able to thaw out enough to get my fingers moving before the conclusion of the lesson.

Ah, Youth!

Sascha Jacobsen

Starting violin studies at age four I had many teachers over the years. My first was my Uncle Dave—a musician born and educated in Russia.

Still in his teens when he arrived in Canada, he met and married my Aunt Sophie. He liked to think of himself as a "modern" man. According to his own definition "modern" meant freedom—freedom from vows, freedom from responsibilities. He remained with my aunt long enough to father four children, three girls and a boy. When the boy was ten days old my Uncle decided it was time to leave.

He chose as his new partner one of the ladies in his "Balalaika" orchestra. My father, (his cousin, as well as his brother-in-law) tried to talk him into returning to responsibilities and reality, but he was not willing to listen nor even to consider the possibility.

I had a total of three lessons with him. The first lesson was wonderful. Uncle Dave showed me how to draw the bow across the strings, taught me the names of each of the four strings, how to hold the violin. Then, as I was drawing the bow across each string Uncle Dave sat down at the piano and played chords—bright chords, dark chords, happy chords, chords that tugged at the heart. I felt as though I were in the midst of a color explosion. Instinctively I managed to do things with the bow that emphasized the color and mood of the chords. Uncle Dave assured my mother that I was a great talent and would go far as a violinist. He assigned complex finger and bow exercises and scheduled me for the next lesson.

The second lesson went reasonably well. Again he assigned more complicated exercises. When my mother and I arrived for the third lesson Uncle Dave was in a very bad mood. He was impatient with me, said unkind things, even shouted at me. I said nothing to him at the time, but as soon as my mother and I were outside the house I put my violin case on the ground, put my hands on my hips, and said, in my best no-nonsense voice: "If *you* want me to study the violin you'll have to find a nice lady teacher who doesn't holler."

My next teacher was Miss Martha Slater, a very nice lady who didn't holler. After Miss Slater's efforts helped me win an all-city competition, my family sent me to Toronto to study with Henri Czaplinski at the Hamburg Conservatory. He was a Paganini-type player. What distinguished him from every other teacher I had—before and after him—was his zeal for editing. Rhythms, harmonies, notes—all were changed—at every lesson and at every whim. He did insist that I come to the Conservatory every day to do my practicing. During the four or five hours I was there he would come in numerous times—to listen, to suggest, to change. Every time I had a formal lesson, once or twice a week he would insist that every one of his students be there to listen. He said he wanted me to get used to playing for audiences.

My next teacher was Ferdinand Fillion, a Frenchman, head of the violin department at the Royal Conservatory in Toronto. I must have learned new technical skills, but was not particularly inspired by him.

My mother, meanwhile, was looking farther afield. She moved the family to Rochester, New York, and managed to get a scholarship for me at the Eastman School. In September of 1925 I began my studies there with Vladimir Reznikoff. Again, I practiced where he could check on my progress and make sure I was learning to use my practice time efficiently. I studied with him for three or four years.

One day there was a knock on the door of our apartment. My mother opened the door. There stood an elegant, charming lady who introduced herself as Mrs. Hazel Stern. She said she'd been given my name by the principal of the school I attended. Could she be of help to Esther in any way—clothes, books, etc.? My mother, despite her struggles with the English language, could be very direct when necessary. "Esther doesn't need clothes. She needs to go to New York to study with the great teacher. She also needs a really good violin."

Mrs. Stern became my caring friend, my devoted, generous patron.

When I left for New York Mrs. Stern promised that if I could win a scholarship at the Damrosch Institute of Musical Art she would take care of my living expenses in New York. I had hoped to audition for lessons with the great Leopold Auer—teacher of every famous violinist of that time—Jascha Heifetz, Mischa Elman, Toscha Seidel, among many. I had played for Victor Kuzdo, one of Auer's numerous assistants. He was eager to have me as a student and offered me a generous partial scholarship. He said Leopold Auer was not accepting any more students.

My mother felt I should play for Sascha Jacobsen at the Institute of Musical Art. I had an appointment set up for me by one of his many admirers who was lavish in his praise of Sascha's musicianship, his impeccable taste, his mastery of the violin, and of the bow.

I played for Mr. Jacobsen at his New York apartment in the East Sixties, near Central Park. I have no recollection of what I wore or how I looked, but his look of surprise, the controlled twinkle in his eyes made me realize I had much to learn about style and good taste.

He asked me a few questions about my teachers, then motioned for me to play. I started to play the usual excerpts, but he interrupted every time "not the slow movement" he'd say. "I want to hear the last movement. in tempo." He commented on a few "adjustments" I made. "That's not the way it's written. You're playing on two strings at once instead of crossing strings". I realized he was on to every one of my many "adjustments". I realized, too, that he would be the kind of teacher who transforms a player into a musician.

He accepted me as his student. He arranged for me to play for Dr. Frank Damrosch, founder of the Institute of Musical Art. My mother went with me. After the audition Damrosch said he would accept me as a full time student at the Institute, with Sascha Jacobsen as my violin teacher. My mother had told him I needed a scholarship for tuition. Damrosch replied that it was the Institute's policy *not* to offer scholarship for the student's first year. "That is because we have to observe how receptive a student is to new ideas, to repertoire, to long term goals, etc."

My mother and I must have looked very somber as Dr. Damrosch continued. "But in this case I feel I am making the right decision in offering Esther a half scholarship for her first year."

From the first lesson with Mr. Jacobsen I realized I was in the presence of a master. Everything he did, everything he asked me to do—served the music. He made me aware of every mark, of every word on the printed music.

Pointing out crescendi, tempo indications and accents, he said, "This is the composer talking to you about his composition. He's saying, "This is how I want it played.""

Leopold Auer's Letter

One day, in a hurry to get to my next class, I left some music in Mr. Jacobsen's room. At four that afternoon I returned to room G to retrieve my music, barged into the room, and there was Leopold Auer, the legendary violin teacher of my generation. He said to me "You have come to play for me?" I was so overcome with awe that I couldn't find my voice. I backed out of the room, almost fell down the stairs, and felt as though I had seen—and heard—a vision.

My parents usually came to the subway station to escort me home. I was so awed at seeing the great Leopold Auer *in person* that I could hardly find the coherent words to tell my parents about it.

At my next lesson with Mr. Jacobsen I brought up the subject. "Do you know who teaches in this very room? Leopold Auer. And he talked to me!"

Sascha seemed to take it in stride. "Oh," he said casually, "I've been meaning to have you play for him." Immediately after the lesson I flew down the stairs to the office and told Miss Frank I had been given permission to play for Leopold Auer.

"Calm down, Esther. We'll arrange it." She gave me a date—and I began to practice longer and harder than I usually did.

The magic day arrived. Promptly at four o'clock Leopold Auer walked into the room. There were four students in the Master Class. Each one was to play for half an hour while the others listened and took notes of the Master's comments. Usually, that was it—the one class with Auer indicating a degree of advancement, of superior talent sufficient to allow the student the prestige of saying "I was chosen to play for Leopold Auer."

After I played he walked over to the music stand, discussed turns and embellishments, phrasing, etc. Then said "And next time you will bring me___." I had a total of twenty lessons with the Master.

One day, while playing for him I had the feeling he was looking me over—more than he was listening. I knew he observed my scuffed shoes, my homemade dress, my non-beauty-parlor styled hairdo. "How is it," he asked without preliminaries, "that you have such a fine violin?"

I told him about Mrs. Stern, who had been my patroness and friend, who sent me to New York to study and, eventually, with Mr. Jacobsen's advice and assistance had purchased the beautiful Landolphi violin for me.

Said Professor Auer, "You will write me her name and address." I promptly did so.

Many years later, Mrs. Stern invited my husband and me (newly married) to meet her in New York for dinner at the Barbizon Plaza where she was staying. It was a very pleasant evening. She and my husband chatted amiably and seemed to enjoy each other's company.

When the waiter brought the check, Michael took it. She reached out her hand to him, saying "If I invited you to dinner at my home you wouldn't think about paying for it. When I'm in New York, you are my invited guests and this, temporarily, is my home. The check, please—and thank you for the gesture."

Weeks later, there was a letter from Mrs. Stern. Enclosed was a hand written letter from Leopold Auer to Mrs. Stern, thanking her for her interest and generosity to me, and mentioning how important was such continued support.

Wrote Mrs. Stern: "I think you should have this letter."

We have it to this day. It is a very precious memento.

The National Orchestral Society

In the early thirties Leon Barzin established his National Orchestral Society as a training course for would-be professional orchestra players. Barzin was a renowned violist, as well as a conductor with an instinctive understanding of every aspect of the conductor's art. To this day his mastery of baton technique remains legendary.

He attracted gifted players from all over the country, chose the best and the brightest—worked them with unrelenting intensity, challenging them with every difficulty of technique, ensemble, and repertoire. Within two years his young players had won positions in every professional orchestra in the country.

Barzin was resourceful about programming. Many internationally renowned artists appeared with his orchestra. I recall a series in which all the Beethoven piano concerts were performed. In another series Mischa Elman played many of the Spohr violin concerti and other neglected works of the violin repertoire.

I auditioned for Barzin in the early '40's. He liked my playing and offered me a good position in the first violin section. I enjoyed the challenge of the repertoire and Barzin's skill-honing demands. I was fully aware of his amazing baton technique inasmuch as I had played for incoming conducting candidates at the Juilliard School. It didn't take long to realize then that every conductor's gesture determines the kind of sound, the precision of the orchestra's response, as well as whether there will be excitement, sustained musical lines, and the indefinable something that makes the difference between good and great.

We rehearsed and played our concerts in Carnegie Hall. Our first scheduled concert featured the Beethoven violin concerto with Joseph Szigeti as soloist. Szigeti was tall and angular. Some critics said he looked as though he were playing in a telephone booth. Nevertheless he was considered one of the most *intellectual* of violin players.

At the rehearsal Szigeti played with such beauty of sound and depth of understanding that everyone in the orchestra as well as Barzin seemed close to tears.

The night of the performance, Szigeti's entrance after the long orchestral tutti seemed harsh and unfocused. At the next entrance his bow hit the strings with such force that it actually dislodged two of the middle strings and pulled them away from the bridge.

Fortunately there was another orchestral long tutti during which Szigeti was able to reposition the strings and retune. There were no further mishaps, but Szigeti did not recapture the soaring elegance of the previous day's playing.

Practice makes perfect—so the saying goes. What the artist really fears are the glitches and gremlins that surface and attack without warning. Practice—and pray.

In the mid forties Barzin inaugurated a series of school concerts with a string quartet—violin, viola, cello and double bass. Barzin was narrator and occasionally, a spur-of-the-moment violin or viola soloist, borrowing the necessary instrument from me or the violist.

Our first concerts were in the Delaware schools—as many as four or five concerts a day in different schools. Barzin would often begin a concert by asking me to demonstrate the range of the violin.

"Miss Schure, play a four-octave scale". At 8:30 in the morning such a command demanded instant and 100% mental and physical co-ordination. It was one way of becoming fully awake in a hurry.

We never knew in advance what Barzin would ask the quartet players to demonstrate. Often he spent considerable time talking about coordination. Then suddenly he would ask one of us to demonstrate *lack* of coordination. Not an easy task for anyone who has spent endless hours on the subtleties of technical control of left hand and bow arm.

In addition to the demonstrations, our string group played excerpts of works ranging from baroque to contemporary. Thanks to Barzin's skills as a conductor, the quartet's entrances and tempo changes were usually exemplary. Nevertheless, we were constantly on the alert. Barzin taught us not *ever* to take anything for granted. Fast tempi were usually playable but sometimes they were will o' the wisp, and faster then greased lighting.

By the end of the day all of us were more tired than we cared to admit. Evenings were for having a quiet dinner somewhere, relaxing, reading—and preparing for the next day's concerts.

Of the weeks' tours I recall only one hotel—an old cavernous building with an enormous lobby and a huge, curving staircase. As we entered the lobby we heard the sound of a piano playing a honky-tonk Kurt Weil tune from the *Three Penny Opera*. My push-button recall brought to mind a scene from Ballet Theatre's *Judgment of Paris* to the same music. I stood there, expressionless, jiggling to the music. Suddenly I was aware of Barzin, sitting on the stairs—watching me and laughing uncontrollably.

Joining Local 802 A.F. of M.

In 1937 I was offered a position with a small chamber group. The remarkable aspect of the offer was that it included payment for the several weeks of the tour. Much as I would have enjoyed playing with them I could not accept the offer. The group's personnel were all members of Local 802 A.F. of M. I was not. Union membership involved an initial fee of one hundred dollars, plus regular annual dues. In the depths of the Great Depression such a fee represented an impossible challenge.

At that time I was playing chamber music regularly and often with Mrs. Cecilia Clementi Pitman. She was an amateur violist whose passion for great chamber music repertoire far exceeded her ability to play. Nevertheless, she assembled her group of players, provided the music (scores and parts), served a delicious, mid-session tea to the players, and guarded me from any attempt to lure me to other groups—even for an evening,

I must say I am grateful for the opportunities she gave me to learn this magnificent chamber music literature. She and her many other amateur player friends knew every note in every score—even if they couldn't play the scores with the skill and passion they deserved.

Often she would invite me to come an hour or more before the session began. I would work with her on the viola parts. Looking over the music, I was more than a little amused to note that she had marked all parts (violin, cello) with the warning "Sh shsh! Viola solo!"

During one of these early sessions I mentioned the offer of a *paying* job—that I could not accept because I was not a union member. I added that the initial fee of one hundred dollars was an insurmountable obstacle as far as I could see. She made no comment. The next time I came to Bronxville to work with her on viola parts she said "We're going to see Mrs. Islin today." She drove us to Riverdale to Mrs. Islin's impressive home. I was introduced to her by Mrs. Pitman. "Esther needs to join Local 802 to be eligible for paying jobs. The initiation fee is one hundred dollars."

Mrs. Islen rose from her chair, went to her desk, and came back with a huge checkbook, (four to six checks on each page). She wrote a check for one hundred dollars and handed it to me.

I said to her "You are more than generous. Much as I appreciate it I cannot accept this unless you let me do something to earn it."

She thought for a moment or two—then said "I have an amateur orchestra that meets here every Monday night." She mentioned the name of the conductor—a well-known reliable clarinetist friend of mine. "We could use your services. You could play with the orchestra and you can give me some lessons. I'll send my chauffeur to pick you up."

Thus I began a weekly session with the orchestra that lasted for more than a year. I might add it was a weekly session in purgatory. The harsh sound, the inaccuracies, the to-the-death fighting over seating, the whole atmosphere of inadequacy combined with intolerance, and—worst of all—the insufferable damage to the music—was more than I could stand. My mother asked "Why are you like a marauding tiger every time you come home from these rehearsals?"

There was one mitigating aspect to all the cacophony and "me first" aspects of the orchestra. I met Dr. Virginia Apgar—a player in the viola section. She offered me a ride home after every rehearsal. A physician—a specialist in treating childhood ailments—active in the formation of the Foundation for Birth Defects research, she epitomized and lived the ideal of making her life a positive force for good.

Unions—Orchestras— Conductors

For a long time, orchestra conductors were as close to being absolute rulers as any king with divine rights. They auditioned prospective players, offered contract terms, season's length, chose the repertoire, (often with suggestions from prominent board members) and conducted all rehearsals and concerts—except for an occasional guest conductor. He could also dismiss any orchestra member at any time for any reason.

This situation began to change in the late forties through the fifties. By the 1960's all the big orchestras were not only fully unionized but orchestra members were able to form committees, hold meetings, make suggestions and/or demands. Contracts contained protections for each player from harassment to grievance procedures. Slowly, players began to ask for standardized rehearsal time, intermissions, health insurance, instrument insurance and vacation with pay. None of these perks were given without much effort and turmoil, many orchestra meetings, committee meetings with management and, oftentimes, strikes or threats of strikes.

It took a long time for many in the audience to realize that each player onstage had devoted many years of study, untold hours of practice before attaining the knowledge and technique to handle every type of music in the modern symphony repertoire with precision, ease, and style. Fortunately for all who love music—player and listener alike—there are dedicated people who work very hard to raise the funds that support the orchestra. Inspiration and the joy of playing divine music was a glorious heaven-sent gift. Unfortunately, this gift did not cover such minor items as rent, food, clothes or medicine.

In subsequent jobs I learned a lot about conductors, music, and the fine points of being alert, watchful, and instantly responsive.

Columbia, S.C. Symphony

In the fall of 1938 I received a call from Miss Crowthers, head of the Juilliard School Placement Bureau. A new symphony orchestra was being formed in Columbia, South Carolina. The conductor, Hans Schwieger, was in New York to audition players for the orchestra. Miss Crowthers had made an appointment for me—would I please go to Steinway Hall on Fifty-seventh Street and play for the maestro?

As scheduled, I appeared at Steinway Hall, was shown to the audition room on the second floor and ushered in to meet the conductor. He asked me to play a variety of solo works, then gave me standard repertoire to sight-read. He offered me a position in the first violin section and explained that the orchestra season length was eleven weeks. The pay was eighteen dollars per week. There was no mention of train-fare rebate, nor any perks such as instrument insurance, health benefits, etc. (These are part of every current symphony contract—and have been for the past twenty or more years.)

I turned down the offer and told Mr. Schwieger that if I had to starve I'd be more comfortable at home in familiar surroundings. After a few minutes' thought he offered me twenty-seven fifty a week but swore me to secrecy. Many of the married men he'd already hired for the orchestra had signed up for eighteen dollars a week!

The train trip from New York City to Columbia, S.C., was long and tiring—at least eighteen hours as I recall. There were probably sleeping car facilities, but inasmuch as I couldn't afford the cost, I didn't make inquiries. Walking through the coaches for exercise in the early morning, I saw the first Jim Crow signs I had ever seen. I felt sad and shaken.

There were probably more than a dozen musicians on the train, though none of us realized it until we disembarked in Columbia. We were met by a welcoming committee consisting of several ladies and one gentleman. I don't remember any of them by name, but all were very cordial and eager to be helpful in finding us places to live. The gentleman may have been a local politician and I decided his role model was Senator Claghorn. He dressed like him, gestured like him and orated like him.

I rented a room in a large ante-bellum house on Green Street. It was a short distance from the U. of S.C. campus. The University's football players had all their meals in the dining room of this house. Since I shared the same table I ate foods laden with starches, gravies and other non-diet type nutrients. My digestion rebelled constantly.

The landlady gave me an enormous room. There were four beds in it. She explained that she had only two other sleep-in boarders at that time, but if more came along I would have to share the room. (I trusted they would be female.) Until then, I had the room to myself. There was a large fireplace in the room. There was also a mouse.

After my first nervous sighting I began to realize it was a friendly mouse. Probably because I wrote many letters in my spare time the scratching of the pen would bring out the mouse. After the first few visits I began to talk to the mouse. "Who invited you here? Are you planning to share the rent? Where is your family?" The mouse never answered back, but seemed content to listen to my chatter. I don't know where his food source was, but he never looked really hungry. I did not keep food in my room. Nevertheless, the mouse was a regular visitor.

In February, springtime came to Columbia. I loved the flowers, the new leaves, the feeling of new beginnings. I thought about going back to New York in April and realized I'd have *two* spring times to enjoy that year.

The orchestra was surprisingly good. There were many fine players including some of the refugees from Nazi Germany. They were coming into the USA by the hundreds. Committees in charge of placing refugees were trying to get them out of New York, sending them all over the country where there were opportunities for jobs, housing, and assimilation into a community.

Occasionally, jealousies and ambitions would surface. The concertmaster was from Vienna. Rumor had it he was an engineer there. The engineers said he was a violinist. Every violinist claimed to be a former concertmaster. Although Hans Schwieger was a fine musician he was *very* German. He insisted that each player be seated five minutes before the start of the rehearsal. No one was allowed to address him directly during a rehearsal. If a player wished to discuss anything with him the player had to make an appointment with Schwieger's secretary.

At the start of each rehearsal Schwieger would stride into the hall, his coat jacket draped over his shoulders, take his place at the podium and announce the name of the composition to be rehearsed. He was fortunate to have some first-class players in the wind and brass choirs. Because of the depression many players were willing to leave New York for a chance to play and keep their skills honed. The quality of the players can be gauged by the fact that at the end of our eleven-week season the first flute player was hired by the Metropolitan Opera, the first bassoon went to the Chicago Symphony as first bassoon. More than half of the members of the Columbia Symphony joined various top-notch orchestras throughout the country.

Achtung! The Aitken, S.C.
Concert

During the Columbia Symphony's eleven-week season the orchestra played an average of two concerts a week. Most were formal evening concerts. A few were given in the public schools—usually mid-morning. The orchestra even traveled to several cities in South Carolina by bus, and with dinner provided by the good ladies of the church where we played. No matter which tour city it was, the dinner was always the same—ham salad, potato salad, rolls and a cold drink. No one complained until the fourth consecutive dinner. The oboe player stood in the center aisle, pounded his cane on the floor and shouted angrily: "I am an artist! This dinner is for peasants!"

The one concert that remains vivid in my memory took place in Aitken, S. C. The town's concert hall was a double-feature movie theatre. Our rehearsal that afternoon was not concerned with the repertoire we were to play, but rather to make sure the stage and lighting were adequate. Neither one was adequate. The stage was too small for the size of the orchestra. There were no overhead lights. Only the footlights gave the players enough light to see the music. It was decided to move the conductor's podium off the stage. A small platform—just big enough for the conductor and his music stand was erected on the other side of the footlights. It was free-standing and had no railings. This meant the conductor would have to step over the footlights to get to the podium—then balance himself while conducting the concert.

The program consisted of the Beethoven *Leonore No. 3 Overture*, the Schubert *Unfinished Symphony*—listed just that way without mentioning its two movements—and the Sibelius "*Finlandia.*" The Russians had gone to war against Finland. Feelings of Americans were all on the side of the brave little Finland. The Sibelius piece was a feature on every orchestra program. Management decided to cover the footlights with tissue paper to add a decorative touch.

The concert began. Schwieger, as usual, walked onstage briskly, leaped over the footlights toward the podium. Unfortunately his left foot scraped the footlights. He landed on the podium but teetered back and forth for a moment before regaining his balance.

He was obviously uneasy on his high perch. The overture went reasonably well until the build-up of the tricky fugue toward the end. The Concertmaster came in too soon, a few of the counting members of the section decided to correct matters—finally the viola section came in with a sound like pile drivers. The overture came to a cacophonous close. Schwieger, somewhat unnerved, decided to go off the podium until the intermission. He took a bow or two—waited a few moments and began the *Unfinished Symphony.* Suddenly someone noticed the tissue paper over the footlights was smoking. There was no choice but to stop the music and remove the tissue paper before it erupted into flames. Stagehands came out, quickly did their job and then the music resumed.

The first movement went well. We started the second movement—a gentle, song-like andante. Gradually we became aware of people in the audience standing up. Schwieger braved a look back at the patrons standing solemnly—and realized it was a show of solidarity with the brave Finnish people. The audience thought it was *Finlandia* we were playing. Wild-eyed by this time, Schwieger continued the second movement of the Schubert. A few of the patrons began to sink back into their seats—finally all who had stood in tribute realized it could not be *Finlandia* we were playing.

When the orchestra did get to the Sibelius work no one in the audience had the nerve to stand up again.

By the time the orchestra boarded the bus to go back to Columbia each member seemed too tired or too embarrassed to do anything but try to catch a little sleep. It was not our finest hour.

Annya

One of my longtime friends was a cellist named Annya Kayaloff. I cannot recall the first time we met. I do remember we were playing in a string quartet. Anna—or Annya—was a fine cellist, professional in her training and her attitude. She was dedicated to music-making on the highest lever. Evidently she liked my playing and my attitude. From that time on we played chamber music, freelance jobs, and kept each other informed of auditions. She and I remained close friends until the end of her life.

Annya was an Armenian, born in Turkey. Sometimes she reminisced about her early years—stories of hunger and terror. One of her oft-told memories was of hiding in a water-filled basement, her belly swollen from starvation. Looking out of the tiny window that faced the street she saw a man shot for stealing a loaf of bread.

"I don't get excited about what Mrs. Vanderbilt has to say about etiquette—whether I should or shouldn't hold up my pinky when I'm drinking a cup of tea—or whether I should tip my soup bowl toward me or away from me when I want that last drop of soup. I have *other* priorities."

Anna had no patience with people who were obsessed with and slavishly observant of "correct" dress, "correct" behavior, or too-careful speech. She once described a mutual friend, dressed "correctly" for some occasion, as reminding her of the Russian maids who would put on all their finery for a religious holiday and suddenly feel so important "both their chins would shake."

Movie plots, especially those in musicals, frustrated her. We went to see *Anchors Away*" one evening. Every time the plot thickened Annya would storm out of her seat and across the whole row of seats. Her comments on the goings-on "Stupid misunderstandings! *He* thinks she means—*She* thinks he means! I have to have a smoke!" Off to the Ladies Room she would go. This happened at least three times during the picture much to the annoyance of the patrons seated in our row of the movie house. Annya came back from her third trip—still muttering about the too-obvious maneuverings of the plot—just in time to witness the grand finale of the picture. All the sailors lined up on the battleship, the two couples re-united at last, and Jose Iturbi seated at a grand piano slightly smaller than the Yankee Stadium.

"Looka dot," she observed. "The whole gahjem Nevvy is interested in their future f ... ing.

Her reaction to Ray Milland's *Lost Week-end* was more personal. The moment the picture was over she jumped up, announced, "Jeezus Christ—I gotta have a drink"—and headed for the nearest bar.

She was just as uninhibited in her personal life long before it became fashionable to indulge in love affairs or even casual sex—let alone admit to them.

She used to lecture me occasionally on my lack of interest in casual dating. "You'll go krezzy (crazy) one of these days. Sex is very important for the nerves. I've had lots of men friends"—and proceeded to go into altogether too much detail. "As long as I feel it's right for me I do it."

She had one put-down for people of colorless personality. "aah" with a grimace—"he was made with the finger."

The Borscht Belt

In the spring of 1938 Dorothy Crowthers sent me to audition for a summer job. The audition took place in one of the many studios in the Carnegie Hall area on West Fifty-seventh Street in New York City. I was in the studio well before the scheduled ten o'clock audition. The pleasant young man in charge asked me to play several concert pieces. As I recall, I played the Rimsky-Korsakoff *Scheherezade* and the *Song of India*, both in arrangements by Fritz Kreisler, a Mozart rondo, a collection of Gypsy melodies, and *Dances* by Tividar Nachez (very popular at that time), also the Debussey *Maiden With Flaxen Hair* in an arrangement by Arthur Hartmann.

The young man was enthusiastic and offered me the job. It was in the Catskills, he said, at a resort hotel called "White Roe Lake." The season was for ten weeks—through Labor Day. I was required to play a solo work at each weekly concert. I would also augment the five piece dance band. We were the "pit band" at their twice-weekly shows—produced and acted by members of the social staff.

Dress for the concerts was formal. The pay, in addition to room and meals, was fifty dollars, payable at the end of the ten weeks season. After a few minutes consideration I accepted the job.

Several weeks later I boarded a bus bound for the Catskills. The weather was humid and oppressive. The temperature was well into the nineties. I began to review some of the many stories I had heard about the Catskills, especially the Borscht Belt. Most of the guests were single girls and some single men. Quite a few more were married men temporarily single for the duration of their stay at White Roe Lake. The women hoped to find a life partner, the men hoped to find a willing partner for the duration of their vacation.

Every person, I was told, had a fantasy about who he or she really was. Most of the men were self-appointed executives or incognito heirs to imaginary fortunes. Many of the women claimed to be personal secretaries to tycoons. I heard, too, that nearly every young woman on a two weeks' vacation at White Roe Lake had spent close to half a year's salary on clothes.

This scenario did little to make me feel I had made a wise decision in accepting the job offer.

A few hours before the Friday evening dinner, the bus arrived at the resort. There were crowds of young men and young women everywhere—strolling on the hotel grounds, seated or standing on the porches that stretched across the main buildings.

As I stepped off the bus I was pleasantly aware of the fresh, clean air. Within a few minutes I was introduced to Julie Weiner, son of the owners of the hotel resort. Julie was the social director in charge of the entertainment department. Comedians, actors, singers, dancers, the dance band—and me. He studied me for a while—my clothes, the circles under my eyes, my travel-weary eighty-five pounds, and my all-too-obvious heavy bronchial cold. I said to him "I don't think I'm right for this place. You need someone who's more glamorous and less serious than I." "Why don't you wait until after you've played for the crowd," he replied. "They might like you a lot—and you might like them."

I was scheduled to play after the dinner hour. Somewhere Julie found a pianist with whom I had a quick, read-through rehearsal. Finally, I was shown to my room. I was to share it with two other girls, already there, unpacked, showered, and dressed for dinner. The room, long and narrow, held three cot-like beds, and a large bureau with three drawers.

Somehow I managed to unpack, shower, and dress in time for dinner. I recall a packed, noisy but pleasant dining room, well dressed men and women. Of the food at that first meal I recall not a thing. It is highly likely that I ate little or nothing—pre-occupied as I was with the upcoming concert.

The large concert room was packed. Someone made a short introductory speech and I played. The audience response from my opening notes to the rousing ovation at the conclusion of my performance, was beyond anything a player could ask for. I caught a glimpse of Julie's face. It was a study in surprised happiness.

I soon learned the routine—the elaborate three meals a day, the exercise classes, the comics' impromptu jokes, skits, or games. Whenever the social staff encountered a small group of guests who seemed at loose ends, at the four o'clock "Culture Hour," Danny Kaye or one of his group would jump in to entertain. *No* guest must ever be allowed to harbor the thought of cutting short his stay at White Roe Lake!

Rainy days were always very demanding of the social staff's time, talents and ingenuity. Frequently the loudspeaker filled the air with wonderful record music—Gershwin's *American in Paris*, for example—a composition then new and exciting in a first-rate recording by Paul Whiteman's orchestra. Violinist Joe

Venuti played the many solo parts with great style and élan. It was an inspiration and an eye-opener for me.

I had numerous opportunities to watch rehearsals for the shows. The young players—many of them recent graduates from the Neighborhood Play-house—were a highly talented group—energetic, alert, equally adept at memorizing lines or improvising whole scenes.

Opera—in any language was no problem. *Rigoletto, La Traviata, Carmen,* were done—to the hilt—in a gibberish distinctly Italian, German, French or Russian. Not all the actions onstage were faithful to the original libretto. Usually, they were close enough to inspire explosive laughter at the hilarious onstage mayhem.

Danny Kaye was the accepted leader. His control of an audience was as sure and effortless as Jascha Heifetz' fabulous bow arm. His innate elegance was a natural foil for much of the onstage earthiness.

Early in the season he decided to "conduct" the five piece dance band. His conducting technique was a blend of ballet, calisthenics, and a quick, sly review of the conducting foibles of many a famous musician. I was his soloist. As soon as I began playing he would turn to the audience, smile, strut, polish his fingernails on his shirt and look pleased beyond words. At one point in my solo I was to play a very harsh, unpleasant note. At the sound Danny would recoil as though struck—hover for a brief moment between disbelief and sadness. Then he would suddenly rise to his full height—a tower of anger, pointing an imperious finger, and order me off the stage. It was a routine that always seemed to please the audience. Nevertheless, for me, playing that ugly note was the most difficult part of the act. I never did get used it.

My favorite time of the week was Saturday night—after the big show. The entire entertainment staff would gather—relaxed, unhurried—for an impromptu review of the week. There were always snacks, soft drinks, and hot drinks. Hilarious stories were the order of the evening, Endless examples of strange requests, strange behavior, strange questions were related and often acted out by these talented people. There was no malice, no intent to harm—just clear observations.

No names were ever mentioned. The actions were so clear it rarely took more than a gesture to evoke instant recognition.

These impromptu get-togethers lasted two or three hours. By that time everyone was completely relaxed, tired from all the non-stop laughter—and ready for a sound, dreamless slumber.

Auditions

Every ambitious orchestra player has learned to upgrade his status by taking auditions—for a better seat in the section, for an orchestra above the status of the one he's in, for better pay, longer seasons, more extras (health care, vacation, and instrument insurance.)

Each local musicians' union is part of a nation-wide American Federation of Musicians. Over the years the AF of M has won many hard-fought battles in the musicians' interests. My recollections of endless rehearsals—without pay—go back to the early 40's. Many a would-be conductor could assemble enough players to rehearse at will. There would be promises of great concerts—with ample pay—in the immediate future. After ten or twelve such rehearsals the players would drop out, one by one, until the conductor realized no one was willing to believe his stories of fame and wealth about to happen.

The unions began to make strict rules about length of rehearsals, intermissions, pay scale, adequate lighting, and safe, clean rehearsal space.

Auditions, too, came under new regulations. There were notices—time, place, and name of orchestra or chamber group. Players were given numbers so that each one was sent in to play in the order in which he arrived. He was treated courteously and given time to play so that he could be fairly judged.

It was not always thus. My cellist friend, Annya, had been urging me, for several weeks, to try out for an opening in the Pittsburgh Symphony. Fritz Reiner, the music director, was in New York for auditions. I finally wrote a note to Reiner and received a call from the contractor "Charley" to appear at Steinway Hall on a given date. He did *not* sound cordial.

On the audition date I was at Steinway Hall well before 9:00 a m—the first one to arrive. The contractor "Charley" greeted the many who arrived in the next half hour or so with warmth and a friendly pat on the back. Obviously he knew most of them well. He had never seen me before—nor I him.

Once the auditions began he sent his friends in one by one. He kept telling me "Don't be nervous, little girl—we'll get to you." I made no reply. It did not take me long to realize he was in no hurry to send me in. I was, in fact, the last one to play for Reiner. As I walked into the room Reiner raised a weary hand. "I don't want to hear any solos," he said. He motioned for the assistant to put the sight-reading excerpt on the stand. Max Goberman, a fine musician as well as a good friend, gave me the tempo (a fast two). Every note had an accidental in front of it.) I had hardly time to put my bow to the string before Reiner waved the weary hand again. "Time for lunch" he said. Max gave me a glance that spoke volumes—sadness at Reiner's callous behavior, anger at the unfairness, and the high-handed dismissal, apology for being unable to correct any of it.

By the time I arrived home I was so tired and discouraged, I was barely able to put the violin away. I had been practicing seven hours a day. Now, after the "audition" I could not tolerate the thought of playing a note. One whole week went by before I began practicing again.

More than half a century later I find it still painful to recollect that day. The Musicians Union has, since that time, formulated rules and regulations that guarantee each player a fair chance. It has been a long, hard struggle but the Union persisted in its aim—dignity as well as material rewards for the musician. No longer can conductors hire and fire at will. Once a player is given a contract he is protected by clearly defined rules. Gone are the days when conductors were absolute rulers of their domain. Now a player's contract offers protection from harassment, the right to appeal any questionable act before a committee of his peers and/or an arbitrator. Although the conductor usually selects the players he thinks will work best in the section, it is nearly always a choice with which the committee concurs.

Working conditions, length of rehearsals, intermissions, pay-scales—all have seen dramatic gains in the players' favor. All are the results of hard-won battles by the Musicians' Union.

USO Tour

In the fall of 1942 I auditioned for a twenty-three week tour of a USO-sponsored symphony orchestra. Its purpose, we were told, was to bring classical music concerts to the troops. The tour was scheduled to play in the Army camps from New England to the Pacific Coast.

As a member of the first violin section I attended several rehearsals in New York before the start of the tour. Robert Zeller was the conductor. At that time many of the young conductors were virtually clones of Leonard Bernstein—in matters of dress, conducting techniques and their approach to the music. What separated many, if not most, of these aspiring maestros was the lack of that indefinable "something" that makes the difference between good and great.

Our soloist was a tall, blond lady soprano who—rumor had it—was married at one time to the manager of the Chicago Opera.

In the beginning of the tour our program consisted of the overture to Mozart's *Marriage of Figaro*, both movements of the Schubert *Unfinished Symphony*, several arias, and, finally, a group of Morton Gould arrangements: *When Johnny Comes Marching Home*, *American Salute* and his *Pavane*.

Between the arias and the Morton Gould pieces we had three Strauss Waltzes—the *Blue Danube*, the *Emperor Waltz*, and the *Tales from the Vienna Woods*. The idea was to give each audience the chance to select the waltz it preferred. For weeks we played in camp after camp where the request was always for the *Blue Danube*. Then, suddenly, it was for the *Emperor Waltz*. A while after that it was for *Tales From the Vienna Woods*.

I think we all grew a little complacent. The repertoire was hardly challenging, the bus trips were tiring, meals in the army chow line were not the stuff of gourmet over-achievers and, worst of all, the accommodations ranged form barely acceptable to totally unacceptable.

The orchestra had been on tour for several weeks when minor irritations exploded into a major blow up. We were rehearsing a Mozart aria with a soloist. She was a well-trained singer, with a reasonably good sense of style.

Zeller's approach to Mozart was a little unsettling. He was in such awe of the composer's genius that—obviously—no mere human being could do justice to it.

The music was too good to be played or sung by mere mortals. Zeller would not let the soloist sing more than a few notes before he would stop her, find fault with phrasing, with style, or with her concept of the aria. After ten minutes of rising tempers and stubborn insistence, the soloist, in a huff, left the stage. Zeller threatened he would not allow her to sing at the concert that evening.

The concert was scheduled that Saturday evening at the Indian Gap Proving Grounds, near Baltimore. The audience was large and very restless. We learned later that the recruits had been *ordered* to attend the concert, that most of them had never heard a concert before, that most, if not all of them, had other ideas on how to spend a Saturday night.

The program began with the *Marriage of Figaro* overture—fast, light, short. It seemed to quiet the audience. Then we began the Schubert *Unfinished*. It had become our custom, some weeks before, to play only the opening movement of the symphony. The second movement, apparently, was more wearing than inspiring for these audiences.

For some strange, unfathomable reason Zeller decided we would play *both* movements at this performance. The audience sat stolidly through the first movement but became increasingly restless as the second movement continued its slow, introspective pace. Suddenly, a few of the recruits could stand it no longer. Moving into the aisles, waving their arms, dancing to some inner music of their own they shouted "C'mon, man, give us some jive." By this time hundreds of them were out of their seats, milling, chanting, cavorting.

For the performers onstage this was a surrealist nightmare—everyone in the orchestra was aware of the potential for uncontrolled mayhem.

Precisely then, in marched Mr. Baldini, the head of the USO performance division. He made his way forcefully down the aisle and to the backstage area. The orchestra members, having somehow, finished the *Unfinished* went backstage for the intermission break—just in time to see and hear Baldini shout "You're fired" at Zeller, then launch into a tirade of accusations and complaints. It was obvious to most of us that the soloist had called Baldini and aired her grievances, as well as any other charges that could add fuel to the fire—or the firing. We never did finish the concert.

Lazlo Halasz

After Zeller was fired we were under the direction of a new (to us) conductor named Laszlo Halasz. He had made a reputation during the La Guardia administration, as the founder of the New York City Opera.

After the first rehearsal he studied the orchestra personnel, particularly the few ladies therein. He decided he didn't need the ladies at the rehearsal. "Ve don't need you" was his tactful dismissal. Within the hour he decided he *did* need us and ordered us back to our chairs. His comments throughout the rehearsal were unnecessarily acerbic but we did go through the program.

His first concerts with us were somewhat tentative, possibly because he was trying out his Master of Ceremonies abilities. His English had a pronounced Hungarian accent. It often caused misunderstandings. We felt there was some hostility from the audience toward him. Whether it was due to his accent, or his lack of humor, or that he was reasonably young and not in uniform was a matter of conjecture.

One afternoon we played for a group of recruits who were recovering from illness or accidents. When Halasz asked for their choice of Strauss Waltz they shouted *Wine, Women and Song*. This was not among our selection of waltzes. Halasz thought about it for a moment, then said, "Ve know you're not allowed to have the first two on base, so ve'll give you the *Blue Danube* instead". The remark evoked a good-humored response from the recruits.

That evening we played another concert at a base some distance away. Again, the waltz of choice was *Wine, Women and Song*. From the purposeful way Halasz took his stance it was obvious the chuckles he'd gotten at the afternoon concert had engendered ideas for a larger response.

"Vell," he said, wagging a finger in their direction, "You know you can't have the first two on this base. So, instead of the vine ve'll give you the *Blue Danube*, and instead of the vimmen ve'll give you the *Tales*.

There followed a long, quiet moment—then the hall erupted. I feel reasonably certain Halasz had no idea of the double entendre; he just seemed happy to know his humor went over big!

I remember the orchestra reaction too. Our first flute player seemed to be getting bubbles out of the instrument. The rest of the orchestra looked as though it had been attacked by a virus that caused uncontrollable shoulder-shaking.

Ballet Theatre Tours

Coast-to-Coast

In the fall of 1943 the Ballet Theatre Company embarked on a coast-to-coast tour, lasting twenty-three weeks. I had auditioned for the position of concertmaster of the tour orchestra. Antal Dorati was the music director. The audition lasted more than an hour. Afterwards, Dorati handed me a huge pile of music. "Come back in three days" he said. "Be prepared to play any part or all of it."

Practicing more than six hours a day I managed to read through all of it, and work over the sections that seemed particularly difficult. The many solo parts in the repertoire were what interested me most. I felt I had to know them well enough to give them style as well as be familiar with the notes.

At the second audition Dorati selected various sections from each work. When he turned to a particularly knotty section of Schoenberg's *Verklaerte Nacht* I told him I hadn't spent as much time on it as it needed. "Why not?" he asked. Nevertheless he awarded me the job.

The Ballet Theatre Company was into its second week of a pre-tour three-week season. The performances were at the old Metropolitan Opera House on Thirty-ninth Street in New York. Many members of the regular Opera House orchestra were hired for the pre-tour season. At that time it was not mandatory that players hired for the tour play the pre-tour Metropolitan season. I was called several times to play performances without rehearsal. The first time, I took a seat at the back of the first violin section. Before we played a note, the personnel manager came to me and said "Dorati wants you up front so he can see how you perform under fire." I assume I passed the test.

The tour orchestra was small—some twenty players—augmented in the bigger cities with local players.

We played in small cities—one-night stands—for the first few weeks. As we headed West to Oregon and Washington, I learned from my stand partner, Isadore Fabisoff, that very early next morning we would be passing one of the spectacular sights in the USA—Crater Lake in Oregon. If I were interested in seeing it, he said, I should ask the Pullman porter to wake me at 5:00 AM.

The porter waked me promptly at 5:00 AM. I dressed hurriedly and went into the observation car. The cigar smoke was so dense I could hardly see through it. Dimly, I was able to discern the card players at the far end of the car. It was obvious that the Sol Hurok Russian regulars had played cards all through the night. It was certainly not my business to tell these aging gentlemen what to do. It was probably their twentieth tour, my very first one. Nevertheless I proceeded to lecture them.

"How many times have you been on these tours? How many times did you take the trouble to learn anything about the cities you were in, or the special features of the surrounding countryside? It makes no difference to you *where* you are. All you care about-or remember-is whether you had a full house or a flush—whether you won a big pot or lost."

Their manners were better than mine. No one challenged me nor chastised me. They just sat there looking at me as though I were a favorite granddaughter. Finally one of them said, admiringly, and in his best Russian-English, "Oy, dot Esster. She spikks such a goot Hainglish!."

Chicago Opera House

New Year's Eve, December 31, 1943. The American Ballet Theatre Company was giving a gala performance at the Chicago Opera House. All the company's stars—Nora Kaye, Eglevsky, Anton Dobin, Johnny Kriza, Jerome Robbins—as well as guest stars, Margot Fonteyn, Moira Schearer, and Frederic Ashton, were scheduled to perform during our ten-day stay in this lively city. After a two-week's schedule of one-night stands, such a reprieve was doubly welcome.

The New Year's Eve Gala had drawn a packed house that seemed to vibrate with enthusiasm. Every performer worth the name responds with his best to such an audience. In this instance players and dancers outdid themselves. By the time the performance was over cheers, "bravi," and sustained applause, it was close to midnight.

As I left the Opera House the sounds of the New Year's revelry, bells, whistles, sirens, and firecrackers, seemed to explode. Waiting for my colleagues, Gertrude and Ruth, to join me for the walk to our hotel, I was suddenly overcome with such feelings of loss and sadness that I began to cry uncontrollably. My brother, Israel Louis, had died on May twenty-sixth of 1943. He was more than a brother to me—he was a caring friend, an advisor, a vigilant protector.

His death was sudden and unexpected. Never one to complain or discuss any subject that could cause anxiety he did not mention shoulder and chest pains that eventually drove him to consult a doctor. Within three weeks he was scheduled for a major operation. He did not discuss that either. On the day of the operation he said "good-bye" and that was the last we ever saw of him. He died on the operating table. The death certificate said the cause was "osteogenic sarcoma."

I was at a friend's house that evening for one of our frequent string quartet sessions. Early on, there was a call from my father urging me to come home at once. As I arrived at the apartment the phone rang. I answered it. An unfamiliar voice said "Well—he died." I stood there holding the phone, repeating, "No, no, no." My father, who had been alerted to the seriousness of the operation, was more prepared than I for the terrible news. He and my sister left for the hospital. Years later he told me that while they waited for the subway train he was suddenly overcome with a weakness, so debilitating he could barely move. The thought of what awaited him at the hospital was more than he could bear.

All these recollections came back to me on that New Year's Eve. Added to the pain of the memories was the thought that I would never see my brother again—never hear his voice, never enjoy his wild sense of humor.

The years have taught me better. I do see his beautiful face, hear his warm, caring voice, remember his anecdotes. These memories have the ability to calm me, to help me be more aware, more caring, make more effort to be my best.

Seattle

Early in 1944 the Ballet Theatre tour arrived in Seattle. The company was booked for a week of performances.

First on the schedule was a rehearsal for the orchestra. Aaron Copland's *Billy the Kid* score, rhythmically complicated, was on the company's agenda for new works to be presented during our stay in Seattle.

For weeks, some of the orchestra members had worried out loud that the rehearsal for *Billy the Kid* would be a trap—a land mine given the trumpet part's difficulties and Antal Dorati's legendary temper. Our first trumpet player—an outgoing, cheerful man of limited English had proved himself a reliable player. He was, however, slow about responding to a suggestion or a command regarding style. His lack of knowledge of the English language was a definite drawback. During the rehearsals in New York there had been many tense moments—due mostly to his deficiency in understanding what was being asked of him. When tense moments threatened to erupt he would smile a lot and keep repeating "Aaay, Maestro. Is gonna be O.K—believe me." Interestingly enough, he did come through at the performances.

The Seattle rehearsal began in a tension-filled atmosphere. The orchestra read through the Copland work with relative ease and virtuoso control from the first trumpet.

At the conclusion of the read-through Dorati leaned toward me (I was concertmaster of the orchestra). "Remind me," he said, "to perform a brain operation on all my first trumpet players".

Lennie

I met Leonard Bernstein for the first time in the spring of 1944. The American Ballet Theatre Company had just returned to New York City after a cross-country tour of eighty-five cities. I was concertmaster of the road orchestra.

The Ballet Theatre was scheduled to play a three-week, post-season engagement at the Metropolitan Opera House. The repertoire would include the premier of *Fancy Free*—choreography by Jerome Robbins, music by Leonard Bernstein.

During the tour Robbins had rehearsed the dancers whenever there was a spare moment. No matter how early the orchestra players would get to the hall of whatever city we were in, the dancers and Robbins were already onstage and rehearsing. I often wondered how the dancers could find the energy for the evening's scheduled program after such a strenuous workout.

Antal Dorati, the music director, usually conducted all the *important* ballets—certainly in the big cities. He was renowned for his ability to shape the music to accommodate the dancers, particularly the solo dancers. He was unerring in his sense of timing, of bringing musical line, color, and excitement to the music. The dancers adored him.

He conducted some of the pre-performance rehearsals of *Fancy Free*, but deferred to Leonard Bernstein for the opening performance.

As we approached the opening date of *Fancy Free*, Dorati gave Bernstein several full rehearsals with the orchestra. At our first rehearsal with him he burst on the scene with such energy the players reacted physically. Everyone sat up, breathed deeply, and played with an excitement that reflected the energy coming from the podium. The music—jazzy, driving, exploding with excitement was challenging and demanding for all of us. I like to think we all felt involved in something very special.

On April 18, 1944, the premiere of *Fancy Free* took place. The Opera House was packed to the roof. When the Robbins-Bernstein began—closed curtains, the sound of an old victrola spinning a Blues record, a lonesome voice—then, suddenly, the orchestra began the hard-driving, jazzy opening of the Bernstein score. The golden curtains opened—and the story of three sailors on a short leave in

New York City unfolded. Jerome Robbins, Johnny Kriza and Hugh Laing were the three sailors. The performance went without a hitch. Dancers, musicians, and conductor gave their very best. When, finally, the great golden curtains came down there was a moment of silence, followed by an explosion of shouting, cheering, stomping and thunderous applause. For one half-hour the curtains rose and fell, the dancers came back onstage for more bows, more whistles, stomping, and cheering from the audience.

It was as though everyone present was determined to savor this very special moment.

The next day every New York newspaper hailed the premiere performance with columns of praise for the choreography, the music, the dancers. The demand for tickets was so great management extended the season by three full weeks. Robbins and Bernstein were now the toast of Broadway.

Fancy Free evolved into a musical, *On the Town*, which later became a movie, as did *West Side Story*.

I worked with Bernstein later, in a Carnegie Hall orchestra program featuring his *Jeremiah Symphony* with Nan Merriman as the vocal soloist. Soon afterward the orchestra recorded the *Symphony*.

The following year Bernstein came to St. Louis as guest conductor and as soloist in the *Ravel Piano Concerto*. Always exuberant, he greeted me with obvious pleasure (much to my orchestra colleague's interest), and called me "Estherke" whenever he addressed me. During his stay in St. Louis he asked to play chamber music (the *Brahms Piano Quintet*), specified a quartet of string players, including me. We played at the home of the music critic of the *St. Louis Post-Dispatch*.

It was a memorable evening, quite unlike any chamber music session I'd ever experienced. Bernstein sang everyone's parts, conducted everyone's entrances, knew every note in the score, *loved* every note in the score. Whatever was lacking in subtlety was more than compensated for in the excitement, the drive, his intoxication with the beauty and power of the music. He wanted *everyone* to feel that way.

Not all the members of the St. Louis Symphony were happy with his enthusiasm and drive. Many of the players—my stand partner among them—had been in the orchestra for many years, and had difficulty responding to and maintaining Bernstein's energy and excitement. There were many times my stand partner would moan "I'm too old for this. You have to be young for these shenanigans!"

The newspapers did, in fact, comment on the shenanigans. One of the papers even printed an editorial titled *Shenanigans on the Podium*.

Sir Thomas Beecham

During the 1944 fall season of the Ballet Theatre at the Metropolitan Opera House, Sir Thomas Beecham was guest conductor for several performances. The ballet he conducted was *Romeo and Juliet* to the music of Delius' *Brigg Fair*, in an adaptation by Sir Thomas.

He was hearty and outgoing in manner and very British in his speech. Before the first rehearsal was halfway through, many of our New York musicians were coloring their native speech with Britishisms. An example: "I say, Maestro, may we have an interval?" Translation: "How about an intermission?"

Beecham was not one to be hurried. The violin part on my stand had a note from an unknown player: "Performance time, fifty minutes. Beecham Time, sixty-five." On the nights he conducted, the *Romeo and Juliet* ballet was first on the program. We began the evening with the playing of the *Star Spangled Banner*. Sir Thomas gave it everything he had, singing along with a great "harr-umph" on each down beat. His conducting was so vigorous that he shook every music stand on every riser—on both sides of the podium. I recall tying to keep my music stand from leaping out of the orchestra pit by holding its base with both my feet. This necessitated my moving forward to the very edge of my chair. On the more vigorous "harr-umphs" I expected to fly out of the pit—along with the stand. The SRO crowd loved every note of his performance. The applause for the anthem was always long and thunderous.

Several years later Sir Thomas was a guest conductor with the St. Louis Symphony Orchestra. I was a violinist with the orchestra at the time. Lady Betty Humby, Sir Thomas' wife, was the soloist in a piano concerto by Fredrick Delius. I remember it to this day as one of the dullest solo works I'd ever heard. Not exactly an audience rouser, the concerto did, nevertheless, receive a fair amount of applause. It was my feeling that audience reception was a measure of thanks for the half-hour nap most of them had enjoyed during the performance.

On a later occasion Sir Thomas was again a guest conductor with the St. Louis Symphony. He was suffering from gout, which made getting on and off the podium a difficult and painful challenge. It was decided, finally, that the stage curtain would be drawn before and after his conducting appearances. Sir Thomas, in his carpet slippers, would shuffle onstage where the stagehands would assist him in getting onto the podium. All orchestra members would be onstage and seated before this maneuver. Then the curtains would be opened. Sir Thomas conducted from a seated position. He took his bows that way as well, inclining his head slightly and extending a hand in a royal-like gesture in response to the applause. The curtains were then drawn and the stagehands assisted Sir Thomas off the podium and into the wings.

St. Louis—Golschmann

In October of 1944 I joined the St. Louis Symphony. I had never played in a major symphony before that time. I knew I could handle any repertoire but was unprepared for the size and scope of the many programs. The year I arrived, Vladimir Golschmann, the conductor, was in his fifteenth year with the orchestra. I shall probably never forget his instructions to the orchestra at the close of the first rehearsal. "Tomorrow's concert—we will do the *Tchaikovsky Fifth* like we always do it." I had never played it before.

My stand partner proved to be a rare find. He told me many stories—orchestra history, information about many an individual player's background and his contributions to the orchestra, in terms of behavior, attitude, and intelligence. He went over the music—pointed out all the places where Golschmann took liberties with the music. "And be prepared for the fast tempi," he added.

I practiced far into the night on the program—particularly the *Tchaikovsky*. At the concert I sat on the edge of my chair and managed to respond to every nuance from the conductor. Next morning I was up early—hard at work on the music for the next program.

The symphony's repertoire was widely varied—from standard works to contemporary blockbusters. Pops concerts and family programs were usually fun to play. Conductors, PR people, and managers tried very hard to find new ideas, "unusual" pieces, new presentations to entice people to these concerts. The Pops concerts often featured soloists or compositions that were definitely off the beaten path. In my first two seasons with the orchestra I had plenty of opportunities to see these ideas take shape.

Larry Adler, the harmonica player, was one of the Pops concert soloists. Justly famous, he drew a large and enthusiastic crowd. Another time we accompanied a tap dancer soloist. The most bizarre concert came about because of the presence in St. Louis of the newly crowned bowling champion of the United States. Ferde Grofe had composed a suite for orchestra—*The Catskill Suite*—wherein one movement was devoted to celebration of Rip Van Wrinkle's bowling prowess.

The decision was made to build a bowling lane onstage. When the music reached the bowling ball sequence the champion was to stride onstage, hit a few strikes and stroll off to tumultuous applause.

None of my colleagues seemed to be bothered by this strange idea. Looking around the orchestra at my talented colleagues I could only reason that there was a gargantuan misuse of resources. Recalling Grofe's *The Grand Canyon Suite* and the *Mississippi Suite* I suggested to one of my colleagues that someone should ask Ferde Grofe to write another suite called *For the Birds* if—that is—he could find a pair of horses with regular habits. Grofe never responded to the suggestion. I guess he couldn't find reliable horses.

St. Louis—Molinari

In those days conductors were not only musical directors of the orchestra but controlled the destiny of every musician in it, as far as the player's job was concerned. Guest conductors were not involved in such decisions. However, some of the more autocratic ones never hesitated to threaten or intimidate any player who did not meet their standards in attitude and quickness of response.

One of the guest conductors, Maestro Molinari, was admired for his musicianship but feared for his legendary temper. He was known for his impatience, his utter disregard of every player's sensibilities.

Whenever he indulged in one of his outbursts, his tentative knowledge of English would desert him entirely, and in his native Italian he would let his temper flare. Once, during the rehearsal of a difficult piece, he became increasingly impatient. Finally he exploded into Italian. He ridiculed the talent and mental competence of every player. He hinted at dark secrets in family history and private lives. He questioned their legitimacy.

Every time he launched into new areas of invective all the Italian-speaking members of the orchestra would blanch, exchange round-eyed glances, then study their shoes. Finally, working himself into a foaming crescendo Molinari turned to the assistant principal cellist and ordered: "Translate!"

The cellist was an Italian gentleman of good manners and quiet refinement. His voice, naturally high pitched, would, under stress, disappear into the stratosphere. He arose at Molinari's command, stood for a moment studying the ceiling, then said in a voice pitched above high "C" "G-g-g-gentlemen, the M-m-m-m-Maestro says p-p-please p-p-play more p-p-piano". Then he sat down and mopped his brow.

49

Esther, Alice and Israel Lewis Schure, circa 1922 (Left)
Esther and Alice Schure, circa 1922 (Right)

Joining St. Louis Symphony, 1944. Esther is being welcomed by Vladimir
Golschman

Esther and musical friends following Symphonette concert, 1960
(Esther is on far right)

Michael Gilbert, Dr. Victor Parsonett, and Esther. New Jersey, 1960

Z D E N E K   M A C A L
Artistic Director and Conductor

May 22, 1994

At this performance we honor a long-standing member of our orchestra family, Assistant Concertmaster ESTHER GILBERT. After thirty-seven years of dedicated service to the New Jersey Symphony Orchestra, she will be retiring at the end of the 1993-94 season.

Esther Gilbert has had an illustrious career. As a true pioneer among professional women musicians, she toured with the Royal Danish Ballet, the Dallas Symphony Orchestra, and the American Ballet Theatre Orchestra where she performed as concertmaster. One of the highlights was performing the debut of *Fancy Free* under the direction of Leonard Bernstein. After her touring years, she joined the St. Louis Symphony Orchestra where she remained for four years prior to moving to New Jersey and joining the NJSO in 1957. Originally from Canada, Esther studied at the Royal Conservatory of Music in Toronto, the Eastman School of Music and the Juilliard School where she obtained her masters degree in music performance. In 1963 the NJSO bestowed upon Esther the distinguished "Note of Triumph" aware for her immeasurable support and service over a period of many years. She shared this award with musicians Genevieve Hall and Hilbert Serbin.

The New Jersey Symphony Orchestra's Board of Trustees, Musicians and Administrative Staff appreciate Esther Gilbert's dedication and would like to thank her for many years of wonderful music. We wish her happiness and success in all of her future endeavors.

NJSO concert announcing Esther's retirement, 1994

May 20, 1994

Dear Esther Gilbert,

If any one person comes to mind when I think of my days with the New Jersey Symphony Orchestra it's my associate concert master Esther Gilbert. You were a symbol of professionalism. Your commitment to the music, to the orchestra, to whoever was conducting was limitless, as limitless as my best wishes to you and yours on this occasion —

Love
Henry

Letter from Henry Lewis, one of NJSO's conductors, upon the occasion of Esther's retirement

Kenneth Schermerhorn
Music Director and Conductor

Steven I. Greil
Executive Director

THE NASHVILLE SYMPHONY
208 23rd Avenue North • Nashville, Tennessee 37203
615 329-3033 • FAX 615 329-2304

May 13, 1994

Ms. Esther Gilbert
The New Jersey Symphony Orchestra
50 Park Place
Newark, NJ 07102-4376

Dear Esther:

    You are precisely what every orchestra needs: a highly skilled violinist, a solid and inspired musician, a dependable leader, an enlightened and refined lover of music and the violin whose devotion and loyalty to your position and craft has been an absolute paradigm.

HOW DARE YOU QUIT?

Much love, as always,

Kenneth D. Schermerhorn
Music Director/Conductor

KDS/fwt

Letter from Kenneth Schermerhorn, past conductor of NJSO

The Disney Channel, Inc.

May 19, 1994

Esther Gilbert
Assistant Concertmaster
New Jersey Symphony Orchestra
50 Park Place
Newark, NJ 07102

Dear Esther,

I wanted to be sure to include my best wishes to you as you retire from the New Jersey
Symphony Orchestra. For me, as I am sure for many others, it is impossible to think of
the NJSO without you. All of us should celebrate your years of great music and dedication
to the Orchestra. Whether in a cold, dark school at 8:30 a.m., a wet field some Summer
night on the bandshell, or in Carnegie Hall, you were always there ready to give your
personal best performance. It is that type of dedication that epitomizes what the New
Jersey Symphony is all about, and you were certainly a role model for many other
musicians as well as one young Orchestra Manager.

I hope you know how much I enjoyed working with you and getting to know you during
my tenure as Orchestra Manager. I admired your devotion to the Orchestra family and your
sense of decency and fairness. I also enjoyed your great stories and always appreciated
your sense of humor. From your experience as a musician, you brought a sense of history
and perspective to the Orchestra that no one else could. That really came clear during our
performances of Bernstein's "Fancy Free," when I realized that you had played at the
premiere and were now playing again with another young, talented conductor. And
then,... there was your wonderful wry smile when things weren't going just as we all had
planned. Perhaps it was a difficult conductor, a poor soloist, or a leaky roof, but you
always were able to smile and go on with the music. Believe me, without that smile, I
don't think I could have made it through a number of difficult situations over the years.

You have certainly earned a special place in all of our hearts. The New Jersey Symphony
Orchestra will not be the same without you, and I join many other friends in wishing you
all the best in the years ahead and hoping that we will see you at future Symphony events.

With all my best wishes,

Sincerely,

Benjamin N. Pyne
Director, National Accounts

427 Madison Avenue, 5th Floor · New York, New York 10022 · 212 735-5393

Part of the Magic of The Walt Disney Company

Letter from Benjamin Pyne, previous assistant manager, NJSO

May 1994

Dear Esther,

Congratulations on an unparalleled thirty-seven years of performance with the New Jersey Symphony Orchestra. You have graced the chair of Assistant Concertmaster with your talent, dedication, and hard work. Your quiet dignity has been a model for all your colleagues, and you have played through all forms of adversity from physical pain to financial uncertainty. Your extraordinary longevity is a tribute to your belief in the New Jersey Symphony and its music making. I will always remember and be grateful for all your help and support. I particularly treasure your encouraging words after performances of Leonard Bernstein's *Fancy Free*. Those words really meant something to me -- coming as they did from the woman who was concertmistress at the world premiere -- with the composer conducting!

Mazel tov! May your retirement by joyful and relaxed -- and free of bus trips to Trenton and beyond!

Love and best wishes always,

Hugh Wolff

Letter from Hugh Wolff, former conductor, NJSO

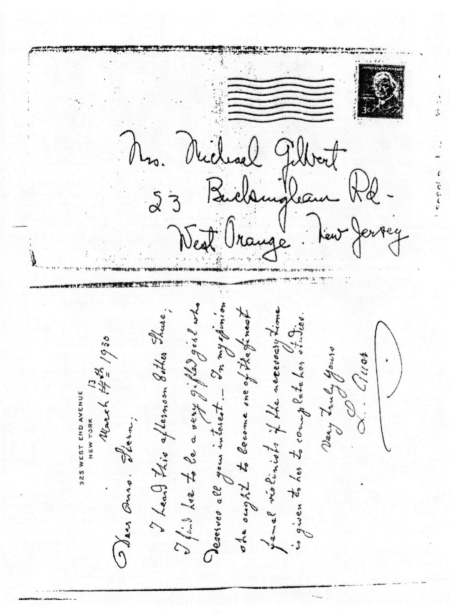

Mrs. Michael Gilbert
23 Buckingham Rd.
West Orange. New Jersey

325 WEST END AVENUE
NEW YORK
March 14th 1936

Dear Mrs. Stern;

I heard this afternoon Esther Stern.

I find her to be a very gifted girl who deserves all your interest.— In my opinion she ought to become one of the finest female violinists if the necessary time is given to her to complete her studies.

Very truly yours
L. Auer

Treasured letter from Leopold Auer

The > **"THE GOOD OLD DAYS" an interview Senza Sordino**
Symphonic
Musician

Most symphonic players will have some idea of what current wages symphony orchestras, but they might not know what "the good old d like. The following story from ICSOM's Senza Sordino is worth shar

"My first experience with a professional orchestra was with the South Symphony in Columbia, South Carolina. It was 1938. The Juilliard p bureau sent me to Steinway Hall to audition for the conductor, Hans Schwieger. He offered me the job—an eleven-week season, no allo train fare from New York to Columbia, and a salary of $18 per week were no benefits for health or instrument insurance. I declined the o thought about it a while, then offered me $25 per week, pointing out who had families were accepting the $18 salary. I accepted—played weeks of challenging works, made friends, played chamber music a home after the eleven weeks with a net savings—after train fare, ro board—of ten dollars.

Back in New York I played a lot of free-lance work. No benefits, no 1943 I played an audition for the position of concertmaster of the Ar Ballet Theatre Orchestra. The audition was at the old Metropolitan C House. Antal Dorati was the principal conductor. I played for him ab hour. He gave me a three-foot-high stack of music and asked me to again in three days. I had never played ballet music before—worked music until 2 a.m. each day—went back on the third day and played again. I got the job. It was a 21-week tour. We played in 85 cities. I per week for 7 performances and extra for matinees. Some weeks v much as $300—but there were no benefits, no insurance, no pensio

I was with the St. Louis Symphony for a total of four years. No comm benefits. When I was with the Dallas Symphony there were stirrings change. A committee was organized and meetings were held at reg intervals.

In 1956 I became a member of the New Jersey Symphony. Rehears $5. Concerts were $25. I was assistant concertmaster for 37 years—unbelievable changes—in committees, benefits, length of season an

I hope some of the bright, talented musicians of today are aware of hard struggle it took to make these benefits happen. Many dedicate gave freely of time, energy and intelligence, despite the risks to job career."

Esther Schure Gilbert, New Jersey Symphony violinist retired

Source: From Senza Sordino, Vol. 39, No. 1 (January 2001). © 200 International Conference of Symphony and Opera Musicians (ICSO permission.

Musicians Union Local 6
116 Ninth Street
San Francisco, CA 94103

Telephone: 415-575-0777
Office Hours: 10:00am to 4:00pm
Dues Department closes at 3:30pm

Join the AFM6 Email List:
[   ] [Join]

Recent article published in *Senza Sordino*

Josef Szigeti

I had heard many good things about Josef Szigeti's artistry as a violinist long before I met him. Most of my colleagues, who had accompanied him when he appeared as soloist with their orchestra, lauded his talents as a musician, as well as a world-class violinist. When he came to St. Louis for solo appearances with the orchestra I was more than eager to hear him.

He was very tall. When he played, his violin seemed like a miniature toy in his hands. His posture was a compromise between his height and the size of the violin. The usual comment from fellow musicians was that he looked as though he were wedged into a telephone booth.

He proved to be a thorough musician—aware of every nuance. Sometimes, at rehearsals, he achieved heights of beauty that were awe-inspiring. He did suffer from nervousness—enough, sometimes, to intrude on his control of the music.

Some soloists become very friendly with the orchestra players, and a sort of camaraderie results. Szigeti seemed to prefer a discreet distance.

Tact and consideration were *not* among his personal traits. Once, as a guest at a party honoring some international celebrity, he was asked if he would like to play some quartets with three of his colleagues. He was *not* pleased when he noticed that Marie Romeat Rosanoff was the cellist, neither did he ask if anyone had any special quartet he'd like to play.

"We'll play the *Ravel Quartet*," he said. The music parts were distributed to the players. "Have you ever played the *Ravel Quartet*?" he asked Marie. (She had been the cellist of the Musical Art Quartet since its inception, had studied in Paris with Pablo Casals, and was widely renowned as an exceptionally gifted cellist.)

Marie made no reply to Szigeti's question. She simply took the Ravel music off the stand, put it on the floor, then proceeded to play the entire quartet part by memory.

Szigeti's accompanist was Leonid Hambro, a pianist widely renowned for his skills and sensitivity. On tours they traveled together, usually by train. The routine was always the same. When the dining car steward announced that the dining car was open for service, Szigeti promptly went to the dining car—but not before leaving Hambro with the order "Keep your eyes on the violin." When Szigeti returned, at his leisure, he would say to Hambro, "You can go now."

He had come to Saint Louis in the mid 1940's to play a Mozart concerto with the St. Louis Symphony. Rehearsals were two and a half hours with a fifteen minute intermission. Dress rehearsals were divided between the soloist and the orchestra, either half, depending on the soloist's preference. Szigeti arrived at the dress rehearsal. Golschman, the conductor, was cheerful and prepared to do all the right things. From the first measure of the soloist's entrance it was evident that the rehearsal was not to go smoothly. Every few notes, Szigeti would stop playing, speak to the conductor, then deliver a monologue on Mozart's style. The rehearsal staggered on and on, inching into intermission time and beyond.

Golschman looked more and more harassed and angry. Suddenly he said "I am sick. I am going home. Harry, (the concertmaster), take over." Harry took over. We never played the piece through—nor did we ever rehearse the orchestra portion of the program. I do *not* recall the concert. I know only that Szigeti was never again invited as soloist during Golschman's tenure as conductor of the St. Louis Symphony.

Grand Rapids

World War II was still going strong in 1944. In any area of endeavor the military had top priority. Travel schedules, train routings, even hotel reservations were all subject to revision or cancellation, if necessary, to speed troop movements at any time.

One snowy day, the Ballet Theatre Company was on a train bound for Grand Rapids. Within sight of the city we were shunted off to a railroad siding—and sat and sat and sat. Finally, the train was given the go-ahead. The company arrived in Grand Rapids an hour after the scheduled performance time. Dinner was out of the question. We all headed directly to the performance site where we found the audience milling about, cheerful—but determined to see the performance.

Dorati, our music director, had received word that the scenery, costumes, etc., would be arriving within the hour, and then would have to be set up for the performance.

The audience was apprised of this—it meant the performance could not begin before 11:00 PM at the earliest. No one made a move to leave. Dorati decided the orchestra would give a pre-performance concert. Within minutes after the music boxes arrived the librarians had unpacked and set out the music for *Swan Lake*, Stravinsky's *Petrouchka*, and *Les Sylphides*, by Chopin.

The audience entered the theatre while we orchestra members took our places in the orchestra pit. Despite the backstage clamor of setting up the scenery, the orchestra and audience rose to the occasion. Dorati, released from the constraints of ballet demands, conducted a memorably musical offering of all the music on the program.

The performance of the scheduled ballets began that night after 11:00 PM and lasted well beyond 1:00 AM. No player complained, and no patron left early.

Lillian Fuchs—Violist

One morning in the mid 1940's I was practicing first-violin quartet parts—Haydn, Mozart, Beethoven—for a quartet session later that evening with three of my colleagues. Much engrossed in the beauty and technical demands of the music, I was startled to hear the doorbell ring.

Opening the door I saw a little, middle-aged lady standing there. "Was that you playing?" she asked in a bright voice. "I could have sworn it was a man." She asked me the name of my teacher. When I said "Sascha Jacobsen" her comment was, "Oh-that explains it." By this time I had recognized her—Lillian Fuchs, the renowned violist. She and her brother, Josef (violinist) had studied with Franz Kneisel, the great teacher and chamber music player of his time. Sascha, his star pupil, assumed Kneisel's place as head of the violin department at Frank Damrosch's "Institute of Musical Art" after Kneisel's death.

Lillian seemed pleased that I recognized her. She told me "I have a special chamber music group that meets every Wednesday afternoon at the Leventritt apartment on Park Avenue. I'll pick you up each week and bring you home." She said she lived "around the corner" on Riverside Drive. My family lived on 152nd Street near Broadway.

Lillian was as good as her word. She stopped by every week for the next two years whenever the class was in session. It was my privilege to learn the chamber music literature under her knowledgeable guidance. The class sessions were widely known by string players—not only in New York, but by internationally known players. Any visiting celebrity in New York on a Wednesday afternoon was likely to show up and participate in these sessions. Isaac Stern joined the group at least two or three times during those two years. He was always a positive participant, radiating good humor and confidence.

I was more than impressed by Lillian Fuchs' knowledge of the chamber music literature. She knew every note in every part—even offered a few suggestions on fingerings to ease difficult or awkward passages—whether for the violinists, violist or cellist.

Strangely enough, I do *not* recall how we got from 152nd St. to Park Avenue. I have no recollection of a motorcar, or a subway. We certainly did not walk. Nevertheless, the Park Avenue apartment and the intensity and excitement of playing these great quartets under Lillian's supervision remain a clear and treasured part of my memory.

"J.H."

In the fall of 1944 several violinists joined the ranks of the St. Louis Symphony. One of them, J.H., made his presence known from the first rehearsal. The moment intermission was announced he made his way to the center stage, close to the conductor's podium, and began practicing the opening measures of the cadenza from the Glazounoff violin concerto. For the entire season he maintained this routine, always practicing the same section of the same concerto in the same center stage spot.

After the first few times the routine became an irritant to many orchestra members—attitudes changed from amused interest to active annoyance. Many times the players plotted to do away with J.H., along with his violin and his bow. Some of the scenarios dreamed up by the plotters were highly ingenious, especially their plans for the bow.

The plotters never managed to *get* J.H., but at the end of the season he was not rehired.

Some years later, on tour with the Sadler Wells Ballet there was J.H. again, still small and wiry, still looking rushed and harassed, his complexion still slightly grey as though he didn't eat or sleep enough.

He began hanging around backstage, especially when Margot Fonteyn was rehearsing. Whether or not she was aware of his lurking presence I can't say. He was still practicing bits of the Glazounoff cadenza and a smattering, occasionally, of the Brahms violin concerto.

He came to me once to ask for a loan of several hundred dollars. He wanted to buy a gift for Fonteyn, he said "to show his esteem for her as a great artist." I told him that even if I had several hundred dollars to spare I did not lend money to colleagues because I liked to stay on friendly terms with them.

When the Royal Ballet made its American debut, there he was again. The concertmaster was a Russian-Israeli. J.H. was his stand partner. They quarreled from the first rehearsal.

Gittelson and I shared the next stand. There was no attempt on Gittleson's part to hide his enjoyment of the constant fighting between the "lead stand" players. Sometimes Gittelson would volunteer a few sly remarks, always guaranteed to fan the flames of the ongoing argument.

We were scheduled for a performance in Omaha. Because of newly added repertoire the conductor called a rehearsal. Again, the arguments between J.H. and his partner continued. Suddenly, in response to J.H.'s incessant complaints that he was never given a chance to play the solo parts the concertmaster said: "You can play tonight. I have a headache."

Gittelson was instantly alert. "I have to get back to the hotel to practice the Swan Lake solos. He'll never play them." J.H.turned to his stand partner and promptly accused him of plotting to embarrass him because "you didn't give me any notice."

When the orchestra began arriving for the evening performance, Gittleson was already there, practicing the Swan Lake solos in the concrete backstage area. J.H.was in the orchestra pit, huddled in the concertmaster's chair, working on the solos. His usual grey complexion was now a pasty green.

Finally, the performance got under way. As the ballet progressed toward the pas de deux J.H. grew noticeably more tense. At last, there were the chords from the harp and the solo began. J.H.'s sound was practically inaudible. The solo's sustained, singing line was sabotaged by J.H.'s bow which leaped, and skipped, and chattered. Half a dozen times Gittleson put his violin under his chin, ready to save the day but, receiving neither recognition nor encouragement from the conductor, decided against it.

Somehow we managed to survive the evening. Once the performance was over J.H. regained his composure. Slowly his complexion changed from green to pale grey; his muscles began to relax.

No one said anything to him about his performance, but that didn't deter him from discussing it for weeks.

For the rest of the tour Gittleson continued to practice the Swan Lake solos. The trombones and trumpets decided one day they'd had enough. They filed into the concrete dressing room area, placed themselves in positions where their every note would reverberate from every wall—then proceeded to play the Swan Lake violin solo with the loudest sound and wildest vibrato I'd ever heard. It was a performance I'll never forget, much as I'd like to—and I think of it every time I hear the Swan Lake music.

Dallas—Chamber Music

During my years with the Dallas Symphony I made it a practice to play as much chamber music as I could crowd into my schedule. It was my antidote for all the damaging factors inherent in orchestra playing—damage to intonation, to the quality of one's sound, to the subtleties of phrasing—to mention only a few of many.

Often, orchestra patrons giving fund-raising parties would ask us to provide the music. More often, a few musicians would get together just for the joy of playing some of the great chamber music repertoire. These sessions enriched all of us—they were therapy, fulfillment, restoration of confidence and affirmation of our love of music.

Sterling Hunkins, principal cellist in Dallas during the 1945-47 seasons, had had a distinguished career in New York before coming to Dallas with his family. His wife, Dorothy Kessner, was a violinist and a long time colleague of mine. Although she was a good violinist, what I recall most about her was her lusty sense of humor. It had enlivened many a dull tour. Sterling's sense of humor was somewhat more restrained, usually couched in more elegant language. It, too, was wildly funny.

In their home there were many books on humor—anthologies, limericks and one, which quickly became my favorite, *American Erotica*.

Once, before a quartet session, I was reading the book while the group unpacked, set up the music stands, adjusted lights and chose several quartets. They were ready to play but I was so engrossed in my reading I did not hear them call me. Suddenly, Sterling's voice reached me. "Don't bother Esther," he said, "She's reading her Bible."

Several weeks later our quartet was invited to the home of a Dr. Wasserman—a radiologist who was also an amateur pianist. He was a renowned cook. Many a fine group of players were happy to be asked to his home. The atmosphere he provided, and the wonderful food, was always part of a memorable evening.

On this particular evening we arrived at his ranch house—a few miles beyond the Dallas city limits—after an afternoon concert with the Dallas Symphony.

The music stands and chairs were set up, the table festive, the ambience definitely *gemutlich*. I was washing my hands in the bathroom when I noticed a large shaker-top container with a label/picture of a very mean-looking rattlesnake. The label read "for use in case of snakebite." I immediately went to Sterling to tell him of my find. "When we're ready to leave I will not walk to the car. Somebody will have to carry me."

Before we started to play quartets Dr. Wasserman, standing on a little balcony that jutted from the second floor, made a charming speech of welcome in his best German/English. He became a little involved at one point, went rambling on for a while and finally wound up with a verbal flourish and a nod to us to begin playing.

Said Sterling: "Now that we've had our Wasserman, let's play."

Play we did—two or three quartets, a movement of a piano quintet with Dr. Wasserman at the piano. Later, there was food—prepared with a master's touch and served with style. Conversations ranged from the ridiculous to the sublime. We listened, we participated, we learned.

British Royal Ballet Tour

Metropolitan Opera House

In September of 1949 the British Royal Ballet came to the USA for a three weeks' engagement at the Metropolitan Opera House. This was to be followed by a twenty-one weeks tour, including Quebec, Canada. The company's principal dancers included the great Margot Fonteyn and Moira Schearer, star of the newly released movie, *The Red Shoes*.

We heard that the demand for tickets far exceeded the supply. The repertoire included full-length presentations of *Swan Lake* and *The Sleeping Beauty* as well as many of the company's specialties. A new full-length ballet scheduled for its American premiere was *Cinderella* with a score by Serge Prokofiev.

I auditioned for Assistant Concertmaster and was awarded the job. Even in retrospect it was a "plum" job—everything from working conditions, travel accommodations, and pay scale were "top-of-the-line."

John Mundy was personnel manager of the Metropolitan Opera. He came to many of the ballet rehearsals and made certain everything was in good order. Two or three days into the rehearsals he came to me and said without preliminaries: "Go to the wardrobe department after rehearsal and try on the page-boy costume. I know how you play. If the costume fits, the job is yours. This is an onstage number for the new Prokofiev ballet."

After the rehearsal I went to the wardrobe department where one of the wardrobe ladies helped me try on the costume, including the buckled shoes. "Perfect!" she said. John Mundy explained that the score called for two violins to play a Gavotte for the ugly stepsister's dancing lesson. "You select your partner. Just make sure she fits the costume. And memorize the music before the next rehearsal."

I thought of several of my musical friends—dismissed them because they were too tall or too wide or couldn't make the schedule of performance dates. Finally, a quartet partner accepted the challenge. The costume fit. All we had to do was memorize the Gavotte.

At that time I was living in an apartment on Fifty-fourth Street and Seventh Avenue. Every time we heard the elevator door open we'd look out to see whether someone was coming toward our door—then ask them if they'd like to hear the Prokofiev Gavotte. Over the next few hours we played the duet for several dozen people—none of whom seemed to mind our impromptu invitation. Most of them thanked us for asking.

When stage rehearsals began we learned when to walk out, where to stand, what signals to expect from the conductor, and how to walk off the stage. Two famous character actor/dancers took the roles of the stepsisters—Robert Hauptman and Frederick Ashton. The *Cinderella* ballet was well received at its first New York performance and was programmed for many performances during the Met's ballet season.

One Sunday afternoon the audience seemed somewhat less responsive than usual to Ashton and Hauptman's comic routines. Whatever the reasons for the audience's lethargy, the dancers were obviously troubled. I was standing in the wings ready to go on when Hauptman and Ashton came sailing into the wings. "F____ the audience," said Ashton, looking livid. Hauptman responded, "Watch your language. There's a nice young lady standing in the wings." Ashton threw me a weary look. "Oh Hell", he said, "If she doesn't know that word by now, she'd better hurry up and learn it."

British Royal Ballet Tour
Cleveland Orchestra Rehearsal
Metropoulis Conducting

Big cities were our oases, especially if the company arrived there after a long stretch of one-night stands. I had looked forward for weeks to being in Cleveland. Several of my colleagues from the St. Louis and Dallas Symphonies were now members of the Cleveland orchestra. I hoped the ballet schedule would allow me time to attend the rehearsal, hear the orchestra, and meet with my colleagues.

John Hollingsworth, one of the conductors of the Royal Ballet, mentioned he was planning to attend. I lost no time telling him about my colleagues. He was kind enough to invite me to go along.

Metropoulis was the guest conductor. Not only did he conduct the scores from memory, but knew the location of every rehearsal letter by heart. Tall, he used expansive gestures—even leaping high into the air at some points. (Hollingsworth, British and elegant, was startled. "My word!") Often Metropoulis leaned back so far one almost expected him to go into a back somersault. He did deep knee bends for sudden pianissimo passages. Sometimes, bent way back, arms stretched heavenward, he gave the impression he was communing with Zeus on Mount Olympus.

At intermission my colleagues joined me for a heartwarming reunion. Afterward, renewed and refreshed, Hollingsworth and I returned to the Ballet routine.

Royal Ballet Train

The 1951 tour of the USA by the British Royal Ballet was unique in that the company had its own private train for the twenty weeks of the tour. Only when the schedule indicated a stay of a week or longer in a given city—Boston, San Francisco, Seattle, etc.—did the company enjoy the luxury of hotel lodgings.

There were many one-night stands that stretched into ten-day periods. Being on a train for sleeping, eating, and bathing could, at best, provide minimum standards for those of us accustomed to showers, bathtubs, and comfortable beds. There were few complaints—mainly because the orchestra salaries were high and the players were chosen, by audition, from a pool of well-known free-lance players.

Nevertheless, weeks into the tour, annoyances began to surface. One of the touchiest subjects was the matter of morning ablutions. The problem was that the men in the orchestra outnumbered the women by three to one. This meant that the men's washroom facilities were inadequate for such a crowd. By contrast, the women's facilities were almost luxurious, inasmuch as there were only five or six of us.

Apparently, one of the men figured that if someone could work out a schedule for access to our room they might alleviate the overcrowding in their facilities. No one objected to this idea. The problem became acute for the usual reasons: greed, impatience, and the "me first" syndrome.

Early one morning we ladies were in the washroom—most of us stripped to the waist, making ourselves as shower-clean as possible, under the circumstances. Suddenly, without an "anybody there?" or even a discreet cough, there were at least half a dozen unshaved, bleary-eyed men, studying us as though we were the intruders. Most of the women screeched and tried to cover themselves. I put on my clothes—my actions speeded by the force of my anger—and bolted into the aisles, shouting for the personnel manager. He appeared in a second or two, took a quick look at me and backed up against the seats. I told him what had happened, along with some highly unflattering remarks about his male contingent and their lack of manners and intelligence.

Said I: "If they can't read English explain to them that "MEN" is a very small word. Only three letters. "Ladies" or "Women" is much longer—5 or 6 letters. If they can see, they'll be able to tell which is their room. They are *not* to enter the ladies room without explicit permission. You are responsible. If this ever happens again, I'll report it to Local 802. Clear?"

It did not happen again.

Spring and Fall Ballet Season at the Met.

From the mid nineteen-forties until the early fifties I was able to augment my symphony earnings by playing the Ballet Theatre season at the Metropolitan Opera House—before and after the symphony season. Antal Dorati, the Ballet Company's music director, had considerable input in the choice of the orchestra's personnel. Many of the players he chose were from the symphonies—Pittsburg, St. Louis, Dallas. Some were players he had worked with on his many coast-to-coast tours in the big cities—Boston, Philadelphia, Chicago, Los Angeles, etc.

Two of these players—violists from the Pittsburgh Symphony—were part of the orchestra at the Metropolitan Opera during the 1945 Ballet Theatre season. Dorati had known and worked with them—at intervals—over several years.

The particular performance, which I recall, happened midseason of a three-week engagement. Normally alert, responsive, accurate—basic "musts" for any of Dorati's musicians—the two evidently relaxed momentarily—enough to miss a slight adjustment in the tempo. Whether they were conversing or otherwise inattentive the result was immediately caught by Dorati. He favored them with his famous glare and personal attention. The ballet finally ended—well under control. On his way out of the pit Dorati stopped at the violists stand and administered a scathing, to-the-point lecture on decorum and 100% professional behavior. Then he stomped out of the pit. After the usual intermission he came back to conduct the next ballet. As he passed their stand, he stopped, momentarily, then took a newspaper from under each arm and handed one to each player.

It may have been a gesture of reconciliation but nevertheless Dorati kept his gaze on the two violists for the rest of the performance.

Leopold Stokowski

Leopold Stokowski was one of the guest conductors scheduled to appear with the St. Louis Symphony during the 1954-55 Season. I had returned to the orchestra after a ten-year interval, and was eagerly awaiting the opportunity to meet and work with this famous musician, conductor, personality, and film star. "What else could he be famous for?" I asked my stand partner—a member of the St. Louis Symphony for twenty-five years. "He's famous for marrying Gloria Vanderbilt," he said.

He then began to give me some idea of Stokowski's rehearsal procedure—a pattern repeated over many guest appearances. "First of all," he said, "he looks over the orchestra personnel and finds someone to pick on. Then he talks about sound. After that he lets the orchestra play awhile, giving the players the full scope of "the hands" display—visions of divine ballerinas, a pleading lover, whispering, rustling moon-lit trees, exploring passion—the works."

"After this he talks about sound again—of how string players are bound and inhibited by regimented bowings. He urges them to use bows freely and without restraint."

All this time he keeps picking on his chosen victim—a little remark here, a suggestion there—registering great patience but very little hope. Suddenly he becomes angry and launches into his "J'accuse" speech. "If you don't want to do as I ask—I don't have to stay here. I have a beautiful wife at home, and two handsome boys. I'd rather be with them."

As luck would have it Stokowski's St. Louis schedule that year coincided with Gloria Vanderbilt and the boys separating themselves from the great Maestro. The newspapers headlined the event on their front page the day of Stokowski's arrival in St. Louis.

My first face-to-face view of Stokowski was a little unsettling. He came onstage—his silver-white hair combed to a high froth—like whipped egg whites. He wore a navy blue shirt, a striped navy blue suit and navy blue suede shoes. My mind instantly registered "Race Track."

My stand partner's account of the rehearsal routine proved absolutely accurate. His victim this time was Erlichmann, the orchestra's highly reliable timpanist, who reacted to the needling with increasing annoyance. Finally came the "the J'accuse" speech—in a honeyed voice that barely concealed his sadness at abuse of his bottomless patience.

"So, Mr. Erlichmann, if you can't do as I ask—or don't want to—I don't have to stay here. I have a beautiful wife and"—his voice trailed off. There was a moment's pause. Then he added, plaintively "Where can I go?" At this point the first flutist leaped to his feet "Maestro, you can come to my house."

I threw a look at my stand partner. He leaned over and whispered, "Please, don't throw up."

Madie Kneisel

In the spring of 1953 I auditioned for Madie Kneisel at her apartment on Riverside Drive in New York. There was an opening for a faculty post for her and one for her string quartet at Blue Hill, Maine. I was eager to see Blue Hill and particularly Kneisel Hall. My teacher, Sascha Jacobsen, often spoke of his summers there with Madie's father, Franz Kneisel. The look on Sascha's face, the nostalgic note in his voice, spoke of a special place and a special time.

The audition went well, despite the fact that her dog, a dachshund, one of a series she owned throughout her life, sat under the dining room table and howled without letup. Madie explained to me that the dachshund reacted that way only "when the playing is very beautiful."

I can't say I was convinced, but was willing to settle for her explanation. I did get the job.

Joseph Fuchs, violinist, and Marie Romaet Rosanoff, cellist, all renowned in their fields, were my distinguished colleagues. Madie Kneisel, daughter of the founder, was music director. She taught occasionally.

What I found most rewarding, summer after summer, was hearing these eager young students at their first class session with the new teacher who would become their friend and mentor as the summer went on. The students were all gifted. Nevertheless, the playing showed enthusiasm and facility, but little else as far as the musical context was concerned. When they played at the marathon concert at summer's end they had become musicians—aware of form, of emotional content, able to bring the music to life with control and understanding. I knew they had acquired a gift that would continue to grow throughout their lives.

For the faculty, the after-the-concert parties Madie Kneisel gave were the fun part of the week. Balsam, Fuchs, and other members of the group would relax, share their stories, and enjoy the good food and drink. Balsam was a delightful raconteur with an unlimited collection of stories. He was, as well, a superb musician and a phenomenal sight-reader.

One evening after a Saturday night concert, Balsam and Nadia Reisenberg decided to sight-read Schubert's piano pieces for four hands. The playing was elegant and flowing. Balsam's wife, Ruth, also a pianist, remarked wryly, "I get so frustrated sometimes. After I've been working on a piece or a concert for months, Artur will come in, sit down at the piano and sight-read it better than I'll *ever* play it."

Balsam told us of a tour with Nathan Milstein in the Scandinavian countries. They played in good halls and wonderful old churches.

In Denmark, Balsam was so inspired and impressed by Milstein's playing that he began to feel he was "already in Heaven." He was brought back to reality in the slow movement of the Sonata by the persistent buzzing of an insect around his ear. Several times he tried to wave the insect away—discreet gestures that did not disturb the music, or the insect. Suddenly, the flying insect landed on Balsam's ear and stung him painfully. With a frantic gesture Balsam tried to hit the insect, but, instead, hit the piano keys with a loud, discordant crash.

Balsam told us "I was sure it was the end of my career. I was sure the audience would rise up and kill me for disrupting such heavenly playing. I was sure that if Milstein didn't kill me he would certainly fire me immediately." Milstein was playing beautifully with his usual style and elegance. There was not a sign that anything untoward had happened. "At the conclusion of the Sonata we bowed and walked off the stage together."

Milstein did not look angry nor did he say a word. We came back onstage for several bows, then went to the green room for the intermission. Milstein looked at Balsam and said *very* casually "Oh, by the way, what happened in the slow movement?"

He started to explain about the insect, how it kept buzzing his ear and then stung him so painfully that he swatted it hard, making a swift, downward motion from the ear to the keyboard, "and my hand hit the keys."

Milstein thought a moment, then said, "You weren't thinking, you should have swatted the insect this way" moving his hand upwards toward his ear.

The Blue Hill summers were a special delight for me. I loved the beauty of the surroundings, and made many friends among the natives of Blue Hill as well as the musicians at Kneisel Hall.

I accepted a contract for my fourth summer at Blue Hill. In June of 1956 I called Madie to ask for a release from my contract.

On July 1, Michael and I were married.

Michael and the Boys

In early April of 1956 the St. Louis Symphony's season was extended for one week. The players were pleased to be recording—at a generous rate of pay—a challenging repertoire including the Shostakovitch *First Symphony*, as well as many works by Debussy and Ravel. Vladimir Golschman, the conductor of the St. Louis Symphony, was justly renowned for his interpretations of the French composers' works.

My sister was not pleased by the orchestra's windfall. She had planned a few social events in my honor. More important, from her point of view, was for me to meet some eligible gentlemen. I was, she insisted, not co-operating. Furthermore, she was beginning to worry about my lack of interest in dating. I tried to explain that I was fortunate to be doing what I enjoyed doing—playing great music in a fine orchestra—proud to be one of the few women in the group. People I met socially, I told her, rarely cared about, or were interested in what was a lifetime consuming passion for me—music.

A few days after returning home I received a phone call. His name, he said, was Michael Gilbert. His sister-in-law had given him my name and phone number. He'd promised her he would call me. "I understand you're a very busy young lady. When are you leaving?" I told him I was leaving for Blue Hill, Maine, in early June for two months. "I'm on the faculty and in the string quartet at Kneisel Hall. In September I go back to St. Louis for the orchestra season. I have a signed contract."

"Well", he said, "I'm sure we can find a free evening to get together before then." We chatted a while longer. I noted the pleasant voice, the clear diction. Finally, we agreed to meet the following Friday. He suggested we meet in New York at the Port Authority building, in front of Hoffritz at six o'clock. I said, "I'm little and blonde. I'll be wearing a black dress with a red grosgrain bow at the neckline." There was a slight pause—then he said, "I'm short and fat and have black hair."

"That's not what I heard," I replied.

Friday finally came. Having to make the trip to New York from Belle Harbor in the Rockaways, I planned to leave in plenty of time. I do *not* like to be late!

A colleague of mine came to Belle Harbor every Friday to teach piano to my young nieces and nephews. My brother and sister lived across the street from each other. My colleague appreciated the convenience and the income. Somehow, he found out I was going into New York that afternoon. He insisted he would gladly drive me into the city. It seemed like a good idea at the time. What I didn't take into consideration was the Friday afternoon traffic over the Marine Parkway Bridge, the tie-ups and traffic snarls every few intersections. Within minutes I realized I would not get to the Port Authority by six o'clock. To compound matters, my friend let me out of the car at the Jerome Avenue subway station in the Bronx. I heard the sound of a departing train as I made my way to the platform. Twenty minutes later I was on a train to the Port Authority station. Once there I entered the building and hurried to find the Hoffritz store. I felt neither calm nor serene when I finally located the store and settled myself close to the big display windows. Forty minutes late!! That's what my watch told me when I glanced at it. I had never been so late in my entire life.

I must have waited at least a few minutes before I noticed someone moving toward me. He was a dark-eyed, dark-haired man of medium height, dressed in quiet tweeds. Michael held out his hand and met my gaze. I can only translate the look that skittered across his face as "Eee-uch."

I decided we would probably get through the evening somehow. Once we left the Port Authority building Michael became more relaxed. He asked me to recommend a favorite restaurant. "You're a sophisticated young lady," he said. "You must know every good restaurant in town."

I explained that when I was on tour I *had* to eat out every day. When I came home for a few weeks I was delighted to be able to eat at home. We stopped at an attractive little bar. Michael ordered a Scotch and soda, then asked what I'd like to drink. "A Manhattan," I said firmly, remembering all the sophisticated movies I'd ever seen. I had not the faintest idea of what was in a Manhattan. When the drinks came I took a sip of mine and asked "Who turned on the lights?" Michael moved my drink to a corner of the bar, and that was the extent of my drinking that evening. We went from the bar to a charming little restaurant named Bertollati in Greenwich Village. Michael studied the menu with me, made some suggestions, then ordered. The food was excellent. Pleased with his steak he insisted that I sample it, and put a neatly carved slice on my plate, then helped himself to some of the excellent veal chop on my plate. Bertollati featured a small but good dance combo and an even smaller dance floor. After a few dances, Michael said he had to get up early to go to work next day, so we had better think about leaving. "Oh, do we have to?" I asked. "I'm having such a good time."

Michael took me home to Belle Harbor. "By the way" he said, "do you know what date this is? Friday the thirteenth." We sat in the car and chatted a while. He said he'd call me soon. I said "I'd like that." Then he drove back to West Orange.

I was staying with my sister, brother-in-law and their children for a few weeks before leaving for my summer engagement. My sister came out of her room and asked me "Well, how was your evening?" "Loverly," I said, and proceeded to my room. She stood there a moment or two, shaking her head and repeating "I don't believe it" several times before going back to her bedroom.

Nearly a week went by before Michael called again. Optimist that I am, I had already concluded "That's that" several days before.

Michael asked me to meet him in New York at Fifth and Thirty-fourth Street. He had the afternoon off and would drive in from work. "Be sure to be on time," he cautioned. "I can't park there." I made sure I was in New York with plenty of time to spare. I stopped in to see my friends, Shirley and Joe Seigelman at Fifty-fourth and Seventh Avenue, then left unhurriedly. What I did *not* count on as I strolled toward Thirty-fourth and Fifth was meeting Mischa Mishikoff, concertmaster of NBC's Toscanini orchestra. I had played quartets at his home a few nights before. He had to tell me how much he'd enjoyed the evening and went into great detail to itemize each piece we'd played and how much I'd contributed to each. I tried to curtail the account, but he was in no mood to be stopped. I did get to Thirty-fourth and Fifth, but not before Michael had circled the blocks four or five times at least. By now he was convinced lateness was a chronic habit of mine. Nevertheless, we had a pleasant day.

He took me to a famous restaurant in Brooklyn, Gage & Tollner's, renowned for its seafood. He ordered, for a starter, clams on the half-shell and insisted I taste one. I had never eaten clams, lobster, or oysters. I was still living in a kosher home, and none of the above-mentioned seafood is considered kosher. Reluctantly, I accepted the clam (which Michael had seasoned to his taste). I can't say whether or not I enjoyed that first taste—I know only that the clam had a mind of its own—it refused to go down quietly and obediently—just stuck halfway. Michael looked as though he'd ruther be somewhere else. I hoped I wouldn't have to be rescued from strangulation. Finally, I managed to swallow the clam. I have no recollection of any taste—just a great feeling of relief to be breathing normally again.

I began to realize in our next few dates that Michael's presence had a calming effect on my restless nature. I simply enjoyed being with him. I liked his sense of humor. I was amazed that the restlessness that summer, always to be consuming me, was gone. I met the boys, Stephen, fifteen, and Richard, age eleven. Michael invited me to come to West Orange for a weekend visit. The boys were lively and interesting. On the second or third such visit Richard brought his thirty-dollar Wurlitzer Stradivarius out of its case. He said "I hear that you play with the St. Louis Symphony. I want to hear you play." I explained that I had a beautiful Landolfi violin—that if he'd bring his violin to Belle Harbor we could play duets.

Richard wasted no words—went upstairs, put a book of music on the stand and handed me the violin. I could not suppress a dismayed "Oh Richard, how could you?" When I saw the inch-thick layer of powdered rosin covering the fingerboard and surrounding varnish. I asked him to bring me some absorbent cotton and a little wood alcohol. Then I spent the next ten minutes cleaning the violin until it was easily recognizable as such. "Now, isn't that better?" I asked, as I handed the violin back to him. Richard pointed to the music stand. "Can you read that?' he asked. The music book was open to an arrangement of "Annie Laurie." How could I not accept such a challenge? I picked up the violin and read "Annie Laurie." By the time I'd finished the piece, Grandpa Dillon and Stephen had both come upstairs, sitting quietly and listening. One thing led to another. After a half-hour I suggested again that they come to Belle Harbor and I'd play on the Landolfi for them.

Michael told me, much later, that when he returned home after taking me to the station both boys said, "Dad, that's the one."

At a Sunday dinner several weeks later we were again gathered around the dining room table. Grandpa Dillon (the boys' maternal grandfather) cooked the dinner. He was a good cook. All the neighbors loved him and taught him many of their cooking secrets, choice dishes, etc. That Sunday he made his special treat, "oven fried chicken." It was an excellent dinner. At one point I noticed Richard was ready for seconds, picked up the chicken platter and handed it toward him. Richard put his hand on the platter and made the following speech: "You're very nice. Why don't you stay here? Daddy has to get up early to go to work so he can't take you all the way to Belle Harbor. He worries about you. So why don't you stay here?"

I replied, "Richard, if you want me to stay here you have to ask your Daddy to get me that little piece of paper. Otherwise the neighbors will talk. You wouldn't want that, would you?"

So began the "C'mon, Dad—get her that piece of paper." Stephen, who had an after-school job, even offered to give Michael the two dollars.

Michael and I were married July First in Rabbi Mozeson's study. When we arrived home Michael said to the boys, "Esther and I were married by Rabbi Mozeson this morning. You will call her "Mother."

"Michael" I protested, "that's a title that has to be earned!" Before I was half-way though the sentence the boys were saying in unison "Oh, but we *want* to!"

Three Classes Music

Soon after I became a member of Local 16—Newark and Essex County—I was asked to play various freelance jobs in the area. Ballet companies, touring road shows, etc. included Newark in their itinerary, often as a first stop on a nationwide tour or, more frequently, as the last stop before a New York engagement.

One of the ballet companies—Moiseev Folk Ballet—was scheduled for a Sunday night performance at the Mosque Theater (later known as Symphony Hall.) The conductor, a Mr. Butnikoff, arrived to rehearse the local players. Having conducted the repertoire an endless number of times and knowing just where new players would experience difficulties with the music, he worked us through most of the program with a minimum of stops or comments. Much of the music was very fast, very folksy, and very hard to read because of the dog-eared pages and fading print. One of the longer pieces was a study in fast tempo changes. As we approached the final pages the orchestra caught the spirit of the swirling, accelerating figures and came to a rousing climax—unfortunately, several beats ahead of the conductor.

Mr. Butnikoff studied the musicians for a moment, took off his glasses, wiped them carefully, and addressed us as follows: "Chentlemen, dohn't help me. I like to play fast, too—and go home early. But the orchestra is not the star of the show. Up there," pointing to the stage "iss the show. In moozick iss tree" holding up three fingers "klasses moozishiens. Forst klass"—one finger "Symphony." "The moozick iss most important—und conductor und moozicians do their best to play vat composer vants. Second klass"—two fingers—"iss opera. Yeees, moozick is important, but if singer is in good voice and high note is in tune, he holds note and you vait. Thord klass"—three fingers—"iss Balyett—lowest! Up there," pointing to the stage, "iss the action. If dancer feels goot, he jumps high—feels not so goot, jumps not so high. Ve play slower or faster. If he make late entrance, ve vait. He makes too soon the entrance, ve jump in. If iss great applause ist beeg success. If no applause iss dezahster! So, chentlemen, please—dohn't help me! Follow the baton!"

Bus Number One

In late March of 1955 the St. Louis Symphony was nearing the end of its annual spring tour. Three large busses comprised our "caravan." A specially appointed bus committee had made all the decisions as to who would ride in which bus—the decisions to be in effect for the entire duration of the tour. Bus Number One—the elite bus—was their choice for the first desk personnel, people who were always on time, and people whose language and decorum could be relied on—even under stress. Besides, by a happy coincidence, none of them smoked. Orchestra members assigned to Bus Numbers Two and Number Three were not impressed. Some of the comments I overheard were hardly flattering.

I was one of the people assigned to Bus Number One. My violist friend, Gertrude, was also on the "preferred" list. There were no discussions—just assignments.

Roanoke, Virginia, was the next to last concert location of the tour. The orchestra was to return to St. Louis the next morning—a Sunday. For some unexplained reason everything seemed to go wrong that Sunday morning. Players forgot instruments or clothes. The bus had to go back several times to pick up players or lost articles. Finally—more than an hour late—we were on our way. Our bus driver felt obliged to make up the time—was driving too fast for the road conditions—light snow over ice. He rounded a narrow curve and smashed the bus into an abutment. Someone shouted, "watch out" but it was too late. The impact was noisy and very abrupt. Players and instruments were flying in all directions. My friend and I, sitting close to the front of the bus were thrown forward, hitting our faces on the seat in front of us—then thrown back, hard, into the seat. Fortunately for all of us, some of the players in the back of the bus realized that we were in a precarious position—just around a sharp curve. Three or four of them rushed out of the bus to flag down any traffic that could be coming toward us.

I looked at Gertrude who was dabbing her eye with a damp handkerchief. "Oh," I said, "You're getting a black eye." Said she "You don't look so hot yourself. You've got a black eye." Apparently the impact of the bus must have caused us to lose consciousness for a moment or two.

We were more fortunate than many of our colleagues. Some of the wind and brass players had dislocated jaws or were missing teeth—both calamitous for wind players. The harpist, who, only shortly before the impact, had been telling us that she never had a filling in a tooth, lost several teeth.

Somehow, within minutes there were ambulances to take us to the hospital. While we were waiting to be examined I heard my name on the loudspeaker—a phone call for me. It was my brother Alex who had heard the news of the bus accident. (The Sunday afternoon New York Philharmonic broadcast was interrupted.) My brother had managed to reach the hospital and get the call through. He said to me "I figured if you could get to the 'phone I'd know you were mobile."

Those of us who were "mobile" were taken to the local Elks Club whose members entertained us as though we were visiting royalty. Gertrude and I were among those sent back to St. Louis that evening. By early morning I had such a collection of aches and pains I could hardly manage to dress myself. I do not recall how we made it from the station to our apartment with our instruments and luggage.

The orchestra's first post-tour rehearsal was scheduled for Thursday morning. Despite black eyes, tailbone bruises and other reminders of the tour we did make it to rehearsal. Newspaper reporters and photographers were there in abundance. Gertrude and I were asked to pose for pictures. Next morning, a little slow in getting to the car, I found Gertrude dabbing her good eye, and laughing so hard she could hardly control herself.

"Wait 'til you see this!" she said—shoving the newspaper toward me. I took a quick look at the picture—two long-faced ladies with matching black eyes—and joined the laughter.

For the next week or more every mail delivery brought copies of the picture, from newspapers all over the country. The UP and AP had picked up the picture from the *N.Y. Times*. Some of the captions were amusing—"An eye for music"—"St. Louis Blues" etc.

The aches and bruises got worse before they got better. At one of the rehearsals my stand partner stood by silently as I tried to ease myself into the chair and, later, just as painfully, tried to get up from the chair. He shook his head—"Listen, Schure" he said finally—"there's only one thing to do. Leave him."

Grandfather's Clock

In addition to subscription concerts, the St. Louis Symphony played several pop concerts series, as well as many concerts for children in the city schools. The orchestra's conductor, Vladimir Golschmann, also provided the commentary. His speech had a pronounced French accent. His stage manners and his dress were in the best possible taste. Whether any of these characteristics helped or hindered was a moot point.

The children's programs—at all age levels—always included a quick demonstration of the orchestra instruments—strings, woodwinds, brass and percussion. This part of the program had been finely honed over the years so that the instruments' color and range were shown clearly and concisely. Inasmuch as we usually gave two performances, to two different audiences at each school, we were on a tight schedule. To accommodate clearing the first audience out of the auditorium, seating the second group took planning and precision. We had to finish the second concert in time for that group to meet its lunch schedule.

The strings were first to demonstrate—one violin would illustrate range and color. Then the viola, cello, and double bass would follow the same routine; then brass, woodwinds and percussion concluded the demonstration.

At one of our first concerts of the 1955-56 season Golschmann called on a new player—a bassoonist—to give a short demonstration. With that invitation the player rose, picked up his music stand and some music along with his bassoon, carried them down to the front of the stage, right next to Golschmann's podium. This took up as much time as the entire demonstration should have used. Our unheeding bassoonist then proceeded to play *Grandfather's Clock* with all repeats and variations. At the conclusion of each segment Golschmann would try to interrupt—politely at first, then with increasing impatience and, finally, utter frustration.

At last the bassoonist picked up his music and his stand and made his way back to the woodwinds' section. By this time we not only had no time for further demonstrations, but were hard pressed to conclude the concert without going into overtime.

Golschmann was livid, the orchestra members wavering between hysteria and hilarity.

For the remainder of the season the orchestra members referred to the bassoonist as *Grandfather's Clock*. Most of them omitted the "l".

He was *not* invited back for a second season.

Frank Scocozza

In mid-season of 1957 I joined the New Jersey Symphony as a member of the first violin section. It was my good fortune to be seated with Frank Scocozza. We soon became good friends as well as stand partners. Frank was a Juilliard graduate, and an experienced musician of impeccable taste. In addition he was gifted with a remarkably keen ear, and a rock-solid sense of rhythm. I was newly married, new to New Jersey. Before the first rehearsal was over Frank and I had established a musical and personal rapport that lasted beyond our fourteen years as stand partners, beyond his resignation from the NJ Symphony, until his death some years later.

By the beginning of the 1960's we had moved to the first stand. Frank was Concertmaster. I was Assistant Concertmaster. I was to remain in that post for thirty-seven years.

During those years I shared the stand with perhaps twenty players. Some came and went with little or no impact, either musical or personal. Some players had strange posture that made for difficult adjustments. I recall one—a tall, thin young man—mainly because he had the peculiar habit of tensing his body whenever we encountered a difficult section in the music we were playing. He would curl inward, then suddenly would shoot his long legs forward as he honed in toward the music stand. It took me very little time to catch on to the pattern. I learned to sit still—hoping he wouldn't knock over the music stand. I learned, too, to keep my knees as far as possible from his side of the stand.

Another partner—of brief tenure—fancied he looked like Nicole Paganini. His mannerisms were carefully geared to enhance this fantasy. I would have preferred he gave more attention to counting. Several of my stand mates felt the weight of their duties to such an extent they were continually interrupting the conductor and the rehearsal. They stood up, turned to face the violin section, and gave instructions in bowings, dynamics, quality of sound. After the first few interruptions players and conductors became increasingly impatient. Eventually there were harsh exchanges, private meetings, and then a new concertmaster.

Decisions on bowings are among the thorniest a concertmaster must make. Every string player has his own ideas of just what bowings will make life easier

90

and enhance the music at the same time. Perhaps the golden rule of orchestral playing is the willingness to make adjustments for the good of the orchestra. Even the most compliant player will, occasionally, have some unkind words for the bowings he's asked to play. Problems are exacerbated when players either can not, nor will not, adjust.

Some times the bowings simply do not work. They get in the way of the music. Good concertmasters catch on quickly. They know how and when to make changes and avoid the rising storm.

Frank Scocozza was able to handle the problems that arose during those years. Although he knew the faults, foibles and strengths of every player he could make necessary suggestions without having them sound like orders. He never descended to personal remarks, no matter how tense the situation.

I was privileged to hear many of his off-the-cuff, off-the-record remarks. They were a sort of running commentary, delivered sotto voce. Their main purpose, I decided, was to relieve the stress of constant control of his "official" words and actions.

Before any conductor was appointed there were many candidates auditioning for the post. Frank had his own method of letting me know what he thought of their efforts. If a conductor's talents were especially modest, Frank would chew gum. One stick—"this poor conductor is not exactly world class." Two sticks—"he needs a lot more training and talent." Three sticks—"hopeless."

Free Lance

Al D'Amico, the principal percussionist of the NJSO, was also the contractor for most of the free-lance musical work that came to the Newark area. Contractors everywhere have considerable power, often hard won, and jealously guarded. As long as they observe union rules regarding pay scale and working conditions, keep track of overtime—if any—they are free to choose whomever they want as a player, as long as the player is a member of the local Musicians' Union.

Sometimes contractors become involved in scandals—kickbacks, personal favors. Al was much too smart to get involved. Nevertheless when he chose a player he always made it seem like a royal dispensation. He never offered a penny above Union scale. After all, the jobs paid twenty-five dollars for rehearsals and concerts. In Newark, in 1957, that was considered good pay.

Montclair College often presented concerts or operas. Al was their contractor. Most of the conductors were chosen from the College music faculty. I recall two of them—one a trombonist, the other a violinist. Both played with the NJSO when extra players were needed. As to their skill as conductors, I can only say that, for the sake of their families' welfare, I was glad they had tenure as faculty members. Fortunately, their numerous shortcomings as conductor did not hinder their choice of repertoire. I recall, for instance, a rehearsal of Aaron Copland's *Appalachian Spring*. Technically and rhythmically difficult, the composition demands skill, discipline, and constant alertness from players and conductor. There were constant stops and starts. One particularly difficult rhythmic section refused to be harnessed. Part of it was in 5/4 time, and very fast. After the tenth try the conductor stopped the orchestra. "You're coming in too soon," he said to me. (I was concertmaster of the orchestra.) "It's in five-one, two, three, four, five (breath); one, two three four, five (breath), etc. I had enough self-control to wait until intermission to explain the difference between five and six—and to point out that music is like a flowing stream. It doesn't stop when you decide to tie your shoelaces or take a breath and not realize you're adding an extra beat.

At another rehearsal the orchestra was playing a Haydn Symphony. From the back of the second violin section there was a sudden, loud dissonance, followed immediately by a shout "That's an E flat!" whereupon a verbal altercation followed. "I *played* an E flat. You're the one who played an E. Where do you get off hollering E flat? You're trying to make it look like *I* was wrong!"

It took some time and effort to calm the two gentlemen involved. Standards—musical and personal—were more relaxed on these free-lance jobs.

NJSO Summer Concerts

In the late 1950's and early 1960's The New Jersey Symphony played a series of free concerts in Branch Brook Park. Usually the conductors were players from the orchestra—the percussionist (and a dispenser of freelance jobs), one of the second violinists (an arts/music teacher from one of the Newark schools) are two who come to mind. The programs featured standard "Pops" fare with an occasional singer or instrumentalist as soloist. The audiences were large and friendly. For most of the players the concerts represented an extra job and the chance to make a little extra money.

What made the concerts interesting and a challenge were extraneous forces—weather, noises from planes and/or exuberant children, flying insects, and, given a windy evening, flying music. I recall one performance where the music was lifted off the stand and wafted into the park, with one of the players giving chase while his stand partner tried valiantly to read the notes from the stand ahead of him. When the player, music in hand, returned to the stage, the friendly audience applauded his efforts. At another concert the soloist was a local lady who sang the "Laughing Song" from Straus' Die Fledermaus." Her efforts to be coy, charming, and feminine were somewhat hampered by a few persistent mannerisms—lifting a leg every time she swooped toward a high note; putting a finger on her chin; making sweeping gestures; lifting her skirt; arching her eyebrows—all, unhappily, lacking in spontaneity and grace.

Inasmuch as the city of Newark was sponsoring these concerts to some degree, the local politicians never lost an opportunity to mount the stage and commandeer the microphone, although I cannot recall any message from them that stayed in my memory. I do remember the numbing lassitude that overcame players and audience. Afterward, it took real discipline to return from daydreaming, to corral ones forces, and concentrate on making music.

Sunday Matinee

Sunday afternoon concerts were a regular subscription series during my forty-year tenure with the New Jersey Symphony. The concerts began at 3:00 PM and were usually finished before 5:00 PM.

On this particular concert in the spring of 1960, the concert began about fifteen minutes later than usual. Whether the delay was caused by a missing player, or a problem with music in a player's folder, I do not recall. Normally a delay was a rare and unlikely occurrence in a professional orchestra's schedule.

Michael and I were invited to a party after the concert. Hosted by a favorite colleague and his wife, I knew it would be an evening of fun, good food, and good drinks—as well as good company.

The concert ended about ten or fifteen minutes later than usual. As soon as Michael could get to the car and meet me across from the concert hall we headed for the party. Almost there, we came to a busy intersection. Although we had the green light there was a large car blocking the intersection. The driver just sat. The light turned red. The light turned green again. Neither the driver nor the car moved. Michael tapped our car horn lightly. I—very annoyed—favored the driver with a full Italian salute—left hand on right shoulder—right arm fully outstretched—and hand vibrato. A moment later the driver got out of his car and came toward Michael.

"Your wife insulted me." he said. Michael—after a brief second—said "She did? Well, fight with her."

The complaining driver stepped back as though he had been hit by a stun gun. He could not find his voice—just stood there, shaking his head in disbelief. He walked back to his car, got in, started the car and drove off. Last we saw of him he was still shaking his head.

The party was a delight.

NJSO—Wolf Trap Farm

Henry Lewis catapulted the New Jersey Symphony into the big time by sheer force of will. Within a year of his making the orchestra fully professional we were giving concerts at Wolf Trap Farm in Reston Virginia, and at the Garden States Arts Center with soloists Joan Sutherland and Marilyn Horne (Henry Lewis' wife at the time). Later that season the orchestra played its first concert at Carnegie Hall—to resounding acclaim.

Transporting the orchestra was an exercise in logistics. Booking hotel rooms for orchestra members, friends, etc. offered its own hurdles.

My husband and a colleague's husband decided to go along to the Washington D. C. area. They stayed in the hotel where all the players were assigned, ate a meal in the dining room, complaining all the while about the food, the slow service, the noise and confusion.

The next morning was a Sunday. Our husbands decided to take "us girls" somewhere else for breakfast—an unhurried, quiet meal before the rehearsal and concert. We started out early enough to be optimistic about ordering a hearty breakfast—waffles, eggs, toast, and English tea in a real teapot.

We traveled some twenty miles, past restaurant after restaurant—McDonalds, Denny's and even one or two that might have had tablecloths and napkins. They were all closed. We learned later that everything was shut down until after church.

By this time, facing a return trip and a 10:00 AM rehearsal, we narrowed our breakfast choices. "A cup of coffee would be nice."

We did not get a cup of coffee or anything else. Back at the rehearsal site with a few minutes to spare, we went looking for a coffee machine. Finding one, I put my money into the slot and waited. The coffee cup dropped down hard, turned on its side. The coffee spilled and splashed over everything and onto my white Mary Jane shoes.

That did it. I reared back and gave the machine a resounding kick. Then I went into the restroom to wash my shoes. I was so annoyed I wasn't even surprised to see a young man standing there looking at me quizzically. I kept muttering about "no breakfast, driving forty miles, every restaurant shut down, and then

96

the coffee machine spilling the coffee over my shoes." I left the restroom with the young man following at a discreet distance.

In the hall the concertmaster, my stand partner, waved to me, saw the young man behind me and said: "Esther, I want you to meet a long-time friend of mine." "We've already met," I told him, "in the men's room."

Henry Lewis

When Henry Lewis was appointed music director of the New Jersey Symphony he took over with explosive force. The year was 1968.

Henry was a man of color—coffee color with lots of cream. Tall, handsome—he was always making the best of his good looks. He wore clothes of the finest quality, beautifully tailored, and the latest style. He spoke in a bass-baritone register, with all the nuances and resonance of a fine singer. His manner and his speech were impeccable.

When Henry took command, the orchestra was still a blend of volunteer players, plus a few union professionals added for the dress rehearsals and concerts. (Payment for the union member professionals was five dollars for the dress rehearsal and twenty-five for a concert. There were no perks—no instrument insurance, no health insurance, no paid vacations—nor did anyone ever imagine a perk such as a pension fund.)

In fact, when any player, speaking informally with an audience member, mentioned such "forbidden" topics as pay or perks the reply was always a surprised, "My dear, you are privileged to play such divine music. That is its own reward." (Strange, how grocery store owners, or collectors of mortgage payments or rent or taxes always demanded real money.)

Most of the volunteer players and most of the professionals held day jobs—school-teachers, painters, plumbers, shoe salesmen. No family could survive on what the symphony could pay.

Henry devoted the first two or three rehearsals to standard repertoire—Beethoven, Brahms, Tchaikovsky, Sibelius, Rimsky-Korsakov—symphonies, overtures, tone poems. We read through them all, without stops or comments. It took Henry very little time to see who could play and who could not. He talked constantly about a "professional" orchestra, "professional" players," and "professional" repertoire.

He did tell us a little about himself. He learned to play the double bass and insisted on striving for the highest standards, musical and instrumental for himself. He was, he claimed, the youngest double bass player—at age fourteen—to audition for and play with the Los Angeles Symphony. The New Jersey Symphony was to see many evidences of Henry's discipline and high standards during his seven-year tenure with the orchestra.

There were soon rising tensions between players and conductor. Henry kept his cool. Many of the players did not. One of my most disturbing memories of that period was of a player disrupting the rehearsal so deliberately and so completely that someone called the police to intervene. (To this day, the memory gives rise to a gall and wormwood taste in my mouth.)

There was a long strike after this incident. When the strike was finally settled Henry had a fully professional orchestra and a daytime schedule of rehearsals. As the orchestra's budget allowed, he added professional players, including several musicians of color—a French horn player, a violinist and a cellist.

Henry was "Mother Hen" to these players. He expected—and demanded—more from them. He watched their attitudes, their clothes, and their manners. Many were the times I heard him lecturing them on the importance of discipline in every aspect of their lives. "Look your best," "Watch your language," "Control your feelings." "You want to *be* somebody? Learn to *be* your best."

Henry was ambitious. Within a season the orchestra was playing at the Garden State Arts Center—summer concerts with Luciano Pavarotti, Joan Sutherland, Marilyn Horne and other famous "stars." Concerts were sold out. The orchestra gave a concert at the United Nations to an international audience of renowned dignitaries. There were many concerts at the Wolf Trap Farms summer festival and several Carnegie Hall concerts, to much excitement and glowing reviews.

Marilyn Horne, then Henry's wife, sang with the orchestra many times. She was not only a great singer but had temperament—and temper—to match. The orchestra enjoyed the artistry and the fireworks the rehearsals always provided.

Lewis had style, dignity, and excitement—all of which were reflected in his music making. He was either loved or hated.

The orchestra's seasons were gradually lengthened from fourteen to twenty-eight weeks. The pay scale rose as well. Nevertheless, the orchestra's growth was marred by divisions among the players. Eventually, the divisions erupted into open revolt. Friends became enemies. When, finally, Henry resigned in 1975 the orchestra was undergoing an inner turmoil of its own.

IBM TV Commercial

The much-publicized extravagances of the Enron affair were the sparks that awakened a memory, dormant for more than a decade.

In November of 1990, the New Jersey Symphony was hired to make a TV commercial for IBM. The pay was generous and promised a fun experience for the orchestra.

The orchestra members were told to bring or wear their evening concert clothes. The service—normally two and one-half hours—might go into overtime.

Rehearsal was scheduled for 11:00 AM. When I arrived at Symphony Hall that morning many of my colleagues were already there. None of them were onstage or backstage, just lounging around in the auditorium. Onstage were half a dozen or more workmen putting a black tarpaper cover on the hall's wooden stage floor. Several hours went by before we were told to go onstage. Each player was given a pair of black socks to wear—no shoes allowed. This was necessary to protect the tarpaper from scuffs. Black linen handkerchiefs were handed to each player. No white handkerchiefs permitted.

As soon as we were seated the announcers and actors took their places near the conductor's podium. The music we were given to play was neither difficult nor unusual. The conductor explained innumerable times, that "co-ordination" was what it was all about. Considering the orchestra experience and stature, all that was required was for the conductor to conduct. Co-ordination would follow immediately.

There were time-consuming conferences between actors, announcers, and conductor. The powerful photo lights were on. Every few seconds—or so it seemed—ladies carrying huge powder puffs, would flit on and off the stage, after daubing noses, foreheads, or cheeks of the onstage, on-camera, perspiring actors.

Intermission time came along. The orchestra had yet to record a note. We were invited to eat and drink. In a large backstage room there was a display of more food and drink than I had ever seen in one place. Mountains of food—bagels, rolls, croissants, rye and pumpernickle bread, cream cheese, cold cuts, salads, cheddar and Swiss cheese in ten pound rounds, crackers, vegetables and dips. Beverages offered were a choice of fruit juices, soda, bottled water, tea and coffee. There was every kind of fruit in season and many exotic, out-of-season varieties. Cakes, cookies and brownies were there in abundance. By the time the orchestra was called back on stage most of the players would have preferred a nap to a rehearsal.

Now the rumors began circulating—every rumor more brazen or senseless than the one before. 1: Another orchestra—the American Symphony—had also been hired, in addition to the NGSO, The decisions were yet to be made as to whether one, or the other, or, possibly, both orchestras would be used for the visual. The same decision would apply to the musical portion—either, or both. Rumor 2: We might be asked to record the entire *Sleeping Beauty* score. (Just a rumor.) Rumor 3: No one person was in charge. (As far as I could tell, *everyone* was in charge, or giving orders, or countermanding previous orders.)

It was a long day. In practical terms that meant that players, actors, stagehands, and conductor, were all on overtime pay. I was exhausted—not by the playing but just trying to figure out how such a complicated, unwieldy, wildly extravagant project could ever have happened. Who could have approved such a disastrous blunder?

I saw the IBM commercial a few times later that month. It was shown in conjunction with a TV airing of *The Nutcracker* with Baryshnikov. There was no orchestra in the commercial, nor any music.

I suspect the Enron CEO's studied with these big spenders. One can learn a lot in a decade.

Ireland

In July of 1990 and again in 1991 the New Jersey Symphony was invited to Ireland for a three weeks' summer music festival in Adair.

By a felicitous coincidence, one of the orchestra trustees, Thomas F. Kane, had purchased and restored a castle and grounds in the village of Adair and opened the castle as a luxurious country hotel.

The logistics of moving a symphony orchestra from Newark to Ireland could be mind-boggling. Fortunately the orchestra's administrative staff, especially Karen Swanson and Susan Scott, undertook the task with such enthusiasm, energy, and intelligence that the move was a model of smooth efficiency. Each morning, at rehearsals intermission, Karen or Susan would give the orchestra members precise instructions regarding luggage, passports, lodgings, schedules, etc. What interested me—sitting at first desk and thus in a position to hear any questions addressed to the person on the podium—was the number of unnecessary questions asked, the constant repetition of the same question—phrased slightly differently each time, and the questions which had been answered in full detail when the information was announced to the orchestra that morning. Neither Karen nor Susan showed impatience at any time. I finally showed temper. "Just tell them it's *not* a perfect world—and an occasional adjustment might be necessary. How are you supposed to know what day it will or won't rain, whether it will be warm or cold on any given day? Will they want a signed guarantee to everything you say?"

Eventually the big day arrived. Luggage had been picked up a day before. Lodging, schedules, passports were all attended to. In addition, accommodations were arranged for family members who wished to go along on the trip.

Management had hosted a champagne reception for all personnel, guests, press, etc., at Kennedy Airport before we boarded the Air Lingus plane.

We were delayed getting started. Our departure time was originally 8:00 PM. Several times we were told to board the plane—then the order was rescinded. By the time we took off it was after 11:00 PM. Dinner was served at midnight. Not many people were able to sleep. By the time we arrived in Shannon, early morning Ireland time, we were a bleary-eyed group. Nevertheless, everyone seemed to perk up in the crisp morning air and the bright sunshine.

We had been told to bring heavy sweaters and boots, that the weather might be cold and rainy. As it turned out, the weather on our first visit was superb—no rain, mild temperatures, and humidity so low we felt invigorated. By the time we were in our second week of perfect weather the maids in the hotel would greet us with "thank you for the "loovely" weather you brought us."

The orchestra stayed in Limerick—some at the Jury's Hotel, some at the Ryan, others in Bed and Breakfasts scattered about town. A few players shared apartments.

In the morning special buses would pick up the musicians and transport them to Adair.

A magnificent tent had been erected on the castle grounds for the three weeks' concert season. The acoustics proved surprisingly good. Rehearsing and playing concerts in the same place was a special treat for the NJSO players whose normal schedule of rehearsals and concerts took them to halls all over the State. It was gratifying to hear how the orchestra's quality of sound and subtleties of ensemble improved dramatically over the three weeks. Hugh Wolff, our conductor, seemed pleased.

Our first two concerts in Adair featured the *Beethoven Ninth Symphony* with soloists and the RTE Philharmonic Choir. The third performance of this program took place at the National Concert Hall in Dublin.

All arrangements for transporting orchestra and equipment had been carefully made. The only miscalculation was in underestimating the traffic conditions in Dublin. It took more than two hours for the buses to maneuver their way from the outskirts of Dublin to the National Concert Hall and Trinity College area. Orchestra members were required to register at Trinity for our overnight stay. Although the staff at Trinity was efficient and alert there was no way of dealing with the sudden crush of 120 people and guests all tired, hungry, and concerned about getting to the hall on time.

Even after registering and getting one's room assignment there was the problem of finding that room in the maze of buildings and pathways. Fortunately there were helpful students who came to the rescue of many of us and escorted us to our room.

By the time we had parked our luggage and changed into concert clothes there was little time to study the room and its contents. My first impression was that it was a Lego model.

Dinner was out of the question. We hurried to the National Concert Hall, left cases and coats in the orchestra room, and went onstage for the concert. Despite fatigue and hunger pangs, the orchestra and everyone involved in the performance found reservoirs of energy and excitement. We did give a rousing concert. The packed-to-the-roof audience responded in kind. Many members of the choir and the audience came over to speak with us with a warmth and appreciation that made the evening very special.

The concert over, the musicians lost no time looking for restaurants or pubs—any place that was still open and served food.

Next morning the symphony management had arranged for the musicians to visit the American Embassy—an elegant house set in a private park. The ambassador was busy elsewhere, but staff members provided a tour, plus food and drink, briefed us on the history of the embassy, and invited us to enjoy the beauties of the garden.

The drawing room contained a magnificent rosewood grand piano—a gift from former ambassador and Mrs. Garret of Baltimore. In the department of coincidences the Garrets were friends and sponsors of my teacher, Sascha Jacobsen, and his Musical Art Quartet, and had presented them with a quartet of Stradivarius instruments for their lifetime use.

I must say I enjoyed this unexpected sample of "it's a small world."

The orchestra's second summer in Ireland offered some contrasts to the first. The weather was mostly raw and cold. There was plenty of rain.

Our Dublin concert was well attended and well received. This time our hotel accommodations were at the Conrad Hilton. Rumor had it that the Persian Gulf War had reduced tourism to such an extent that even luxury hotels like the Conrad Hilton were willing to book tour groups at a reduced rate. The symphony players did enjoy this unexpected luxury.

Our schedule offered us a couple of free days. Many of the players decided to stay in Dublin and do some sightseeing from that base.

The three weeks flew by. Again we packed luggage and instruments and, thanks to Karen and Susan's efficient instructions, were back at Shannon. Soon thereafter we landed at JFK and reality.

Michael made good use of his time in Ireland. Whenever I was busy with rehearsals and/or concerts he would take a bus or a train to some of the beautiful towns and countryside—Dingle, Cork, Galway, the seacoast, ("wild!" he said.).

We have several albums of his photographs of our visits to Ireland. They capture some of the beauties of the areas we saw, and refresh memories of the warmth of the people we met, and of how much we enjoyed all of it.

Retirement

Over the years I had watched as friends and colleagues retired from teaching, from concert playing, and from orchestras. I was often sorry to see them leave but, other than that, did not give the matter much thought.

In the mid 1990's I had the first inkling that I should begin to consider this unthinkable thought. My eyes were beginning to play tricks with notes and rhythms when I was sight-reading. Although my responses were still clear and accurate, I did have the occasional moment of doubt—not a good thing for a reliable player.

By mid-season of 1994 I decided it was time to make my retirement plans known to the orchestra management. I hoped to play until the end of the spring season of 1994. Management and colleagues were more than gracious—each and every one saying all the things that nourish a sagging ego.

On the day of my official retirement, management of the New Jersey Symphony provided a top-of-the-line party, complete with delicious foods—canapés, olives, finger salads, dainty sandwiches, plus drinks of every kind of juice, to the bottle of fine champagne that topped the occasion. Management had been in contact with every living conductor for whom I had ever played. There were letters from Henry Lewis, Kenneth Schermerhorn, and Hugh Wolff.

It is now twelve years since my retirement. Although I miss the excitement and challenge of a performance, I have learned to enjoy the pleasures of leisure. Michael and I moved from West Orange to Huntsville, Alabama, in February of 1999, at the urging of our son, Stephen, and daughter-in-law, Susan.

It has been an ongoing adjustment for me. Michael has loved Alabama and Huntsville from the first moment of our arrival.

Author Bio

Esther Schure Gilbert

Esther Schure was destined to become a violinist. From the first time her mother placed a violin in her four-year old hands she knew this was to be her calling. With great sacrifices from her immigrant family she became a true professional, her career spanning most of the twentieth century.

She received the Hamilton, Ontario, All-City Medal as well as the Toronto All-City Medal, studied at the Eastman School of Music, Rochester, New York, and finally the Institute of Musical Art, predecessor of the Juilliard School of Music in New York City.

Her primary teacher was the well-known Sascha Jacobsen, and later Leopold Auer whose pupils included Jascha Heifetz and Mischa Elman.

Esther was one of the earliest female violinists to play professionally and achieved the rank of first chair violinist with both the St. Louis Symphony and the New Jersey Symphony Orchestra. She also played under the batons of some of the century's most famous conductors, including Leopold Stokowski, Leonard Bernstein, and an eighty-five city tour with the American Ballet Theatre with Antal Dorati, plus many others.

Esther is now retired and living in Huntsville, Alabama.

978-0-595-41875-6
0-595-41875-9

LaVergne, TN USA
02 November 2009
162746LV00005B/56/A